This book belongs to ...

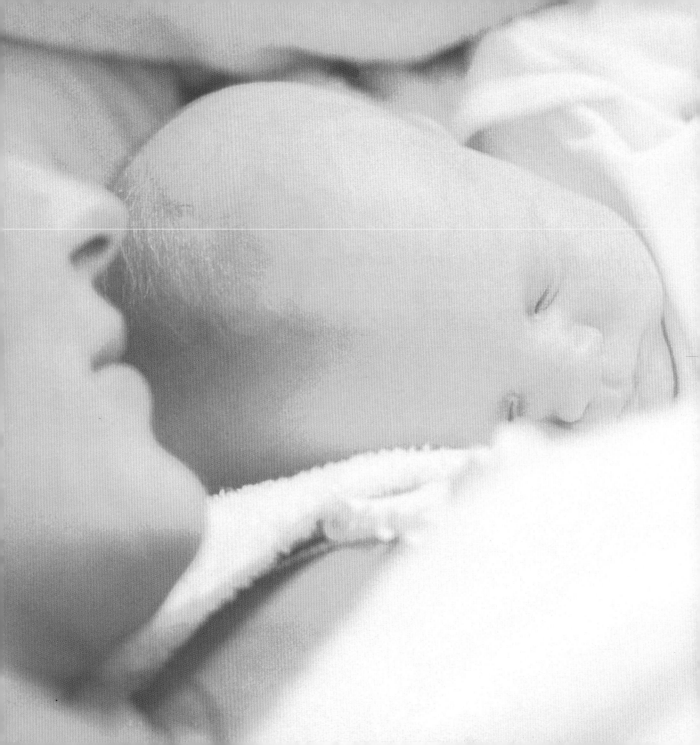

Bless The Baby

MELANIE WAXMAN

CARROLL & BROWN PUBLISHERS LIMITED

This book is dedicated to my mother, Patricia Ann Brown.
Thanks Mum for your love and support.

First published in the United Kingdom in 2001 by:
Carroll & Brown Publishers Limited
20 Lonsdale Road
London NW6 6RD

Managing Editor: Nikki Sims
Editorial Assistant: Charlotte Beech
Art Editor: Evie Loizides
Photographers: Jules Selmes, David Murray

Text © Melanie Waxman 2001
Layout and compilation © Carroll & Brown 2001

A CIP catalogue record for this book is available from the British Library.
ISBN 1-903258-15-4

Reproduced by Rali S.A.
Printed and bound in India by Ajanta

The moral right of Melanie Waxman to be identified as the author of this
work has been asserted in accordance with the Copyright, Designs and Patents Act of 1988.

Becoming a mother is the most creative and awe-inspiring experience in life. The nurturing of the spirit from the time of conception to birth is the beginning of a baby's education, and one that will give him a strong and secure start in life. This has been the understanding of all 'long-standing' cultures. The loving environment in which the baby develops will nourish him on all levels – physically, spiritually, socially and emotionally.

I have gone through seven pregnancies. Each one was different and unique. I was three weeks past due in my first pregnancy and was talking to a close friend, Reverend Tanaka, who was a Buddhist priest. He explained to me that the baby wasn't coming because I was thinking and worrying too much. He offered to perform a special ceremony to dissolve this anxiety and speed the baby's arrival: I lay on my bed and he chanted over my belly for at least an hour. I felt completely relaxed and weighed down as though I was part of the bed. After another hour my waters broke, and four and a half hours later my daughter Alisa was born. During the ceremony, Reverend Tanaka told me that she had a very peaceful spirit and she proved to be a lovely, quiet baby.

We all have the ability to trust our intuition and to have faith in a force that is far larger than our physical world. A force that allows a spirit to choose his parents, choose his time of birth and to feel excited about coming into this world. As mothers we can choose to create a loving and secure environment for our babies and to give them the love and joy they deserve. The use of beautiful, simple ceremonies, natural activities and ancient traditions will surround your baby with the positive vibrations that can help him to look forward to coming into this world. They can make you feel happy and soothed in your pregnancy, too. I encourage you to relish your pregnancy and the developing relationship with your baby. This is the start of a new life full of enchantment, wonder and love.

Melanie Waxman

Welcoming Your Baby …

Looking After Your Baby …

Lullabies and Goodnights …

Learning About Your Baby …

Boy or Girl?

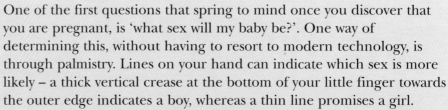

One of the first questions that spring to mind once you discover that you are pregnant, is 'what sex will my baby be?'. One way of determining this, without having to resort to modern technology, is through palmistry. Lines on your hand can indicate which sex is more likely – a thick vertical crease at the bottom of your little finger towards the outer edge indicates a boy, whereas a thin line promises a girl.

Another popular method, pendulum dowsing uses an object of personal importance – traditionally this was a wedding ring – tied to a ribbon or cord. This is suspended over your pregnant belly or your hand (palm facing down). If the object swings clockwise it will be a boy, anticlockwise indicates a girl. Another variation is that if it swings in an oval or circular motion it will be a girl, whereas if it swings in a straight line you are expecting a boy. You are more likely to meet with a successful prediction if you douse towards the end of your pregnancy.

Ooscopy is a process of divination that uses fertile bird eggs. It was first described by the Roman historian Suetonius of a pregnant woman whose name was Livia. She was anxious to know whether she would be the mother of a boy or a girl. She took an egg and kept it warm in her bosom until a chick came forth with a beautiful cockscomb, pronouncing that she would have a baby boy.

One for sorrow,
Two for joy,
Three for a girl,
Four for a boy,
Five for silver,
Six for gold,
Seven for a secret
never to be told.

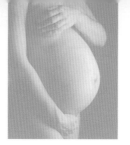

A SACRED VESSEL ...

Windows on the Womb

Meditation and prayer are ways in which you can connect with your spiritual source and learn to trust your own inner wisdom and intuition. Through meditation you become quiet with yourself and can start to block out the endless stream of thoughts that prevent you from aligning with the higher self. The more you are able to trust and believe in who you are, the fuller, richer and more satisfying your life will become.

During pregnancy, it is easy to have fears and worries about your unborn child. The babe in the womb is aware of his environment and is affected by your moods and emotions. Practising simple visualisations and affirmations can help you to feel more relaxed and calm as well as putting you in touch with your baby's spirit. Using such techniques, you can develop a positive and loving way of viewing your life and the world. If you feel happy and positive, your baby will, too.

You do not have to meditate for long periods at a time; the visualisations and affirmations given on the following pages take only a few minutes. The idea is to be consistent and to fit meditating into your lifestyle; only you can give yourself time. Sitting quietly for a few minutes every day can recharge your batteries and make for a smooth-running day. Plus, it can help you more readily cope with the physical and emotional changes that pregnancy brings.

Meditation is also a way in which you can communicate with your baby. You can surround him in loving light, and he will receive your love and a sense of peace through your positive vibrations. Such an intimate start will help to bring about a joyful and wonderful pregnancy and birth, setting the stage for a healthy relationship between you and your baby.

Below are some ideas for meditations, each with an accompanying visualisation exercise to relax you and a phrase to repeat during your meditation – an affirmation. You can perform these anywhere as long as you find a quiet spot. Sit comfortably and listen to your breathing. Breathe slowly and focus on the out breath.

The Spirit of Wonder

Nature is a never-ending source of variable and remarkable splendour. Everywhere you look, you can find something of wondrous beauty. Take time each day to walk in a local park or sit outside and 'drink in' the surrounding scenery, changing weather and the seasonal flora or fauna. Even if you live in a large town or city, you can walk to local shops and absorb all the small, usually overlooked details in everything around you. Practise walking slowly and describe to your baby everything that you see. Develop the spirit of wonder in all that surrounds you.

Visualisation

Start to imagine that you are in a beautiful place. It could be a garden, by the sea or in the mountains. Imagine how it looks, how you feel there, and the different fragrances and colours. Relax into your place and enjoy the quiet. When you are ready, slowly return to the present.

Affirmation

I surround myself and my baby with a bright protective light at all times.

Beauty, Peace, Energy, Calm

The Spirit of Love

The worries that many women experience when they are pregnant are related to a feeling that they alone carry the responsibility for their unborn babies. Learning to trust and have faith in a higher power replaces that sensation of aloneness with a feeling of unconditional love. You do not need to prove anything; all that you hope for is already here. The more you feel connected to the divine source, the less you have to fear and the more loving you will feel towards your baby and others.

Visualisation

Begin to breathe in unconditional love and breathe out fear. You can use the words 'beauty', 'peace', 'energy', 'calm', 'joy' or 'vitality' or develop others that have a specific meaning for you. Feel these words flow throughout your body. As you breathe out, let go of any negative thoughts such as anger, resentment, tiredness, worry, depression, terror, loneliness or sadness. Imagine them drifting away like a river. Continue focusing on your breathing and notice how relaxed and joyful you feel.

Affirmation

I accept any fears and anxieties that I have about being pregnant and becoming a mother. I open my heart to receive all the love that is offered to me.

The Spirit of Gratitude

Count your blessings, literally. Every night before you go to bed, remember all the blessings you have been given during the day. These can be very simple – a friendly chat with a neighbour or a telephone call from a well-loved friend. Give thanks for the gift of pregnancy and for other family members, for nature, for having a lovely home, for your health and for the challenges that life brings. You can also write down your list of blessings and add to it every day. When you rise in the morning give thanks for the new day and all the joy it will bring. Living with a sense of gratitude will make you feel more positive and happy; it will feed your experience of abundance and love. If you focus on what is missing or denied, you will feel more deficient and negative.

Visualisation

Start to focus on your heart and imagine it as a bright sun that expands to consume all of your troubles. Allow this sun to become bigger and bigger until it floods your entire being. Then see the light flowing from you to help everyone you love.

Affirmation

Today, I will empower all that is good in myself, my baby and my life. I am willing to release or let go of negative emotions and replace them with positive ones.

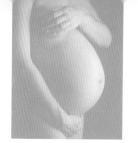

A SACRED VESSEL ...
WINDOWS ON THE WOMB

The Spirit of Plenty

You are worthy of all the abundance that life has to offer. Look around and notice the plentiful nature that exists in the universe and the thrill of its endless creation. This abundance comes from the same energy that created you. There is no separation. Become a willing recipient of life's bountiful gifts and begin to see them showing up in your life. You deserve a glowing pregnancy and a healthy, beautiful baby. Practise doing what you love and love what you are doing every single day. Add something lovely to your life; buy yourself a present – flowers, candles or a special book. Rifle through some albums to find a photo of a place that is meaningful and hang it where you can look at it each day.

Visualisation

Begin to visualise yourself happy and healthy in your pregnancy. Picture your wonderful baby and how happy you feel as a mother. Keep this mental picture clear and uppermost in your mind, and imagine that it is already in creation. Use the present tense in your image such as 'I am' rather than 'I would like to be'. After you have finished, let go and allow the energy of spirit to transform into the energy of matter. Continue your day trusting that your higher power is at work and act as if you already have what you would like to attract. Repeat this exercise on a daily basis throughout your pregnancy.

Affirmation

I see myself and my baby in radiant health throughout my pregnancy.

The world has no such flowers in any land,
And no such pearl in any gulf the sea,
As any babe on any mother's knee.

The Spirit of Sound

The energy of sound can create positive changes in every area of life. Prayers and chants are sung and spoken in churches, temples and mosques all around the world. Some people chant for relaxation or for healing, while others use the spoken word to contact God and the infinite. It is okay to ask for help; no need is too small or too great. When you take responsibility for your need, you are giving permission for your needs to be met. Your part is then to let go in faith. Repeating a prayer or chant strengthens the power of the request and boosts the vibrational charge that aligns you with your higher power. It also stops the mental chatter that prevents you from aligning with your inner self.

Chant

Sit quietly, relax and breathe slowly. Take a deeper, longer breath and as you exhale say out loud 'aom.' The sound is 'aaaahOmmm'. Take another deep breath and repeat. Continue this chanting for as long as you feel comfortable. Aom is a universal sound – 'ah' signifies openness and the sound of creation, whereas 'om' or 'um' represents gratitude.

Affirmation

I will practise the belief that my needs during pregnancy will be met. I'll join in harmony with higher powers knowing that my baby and I count.

When practising meditation, prayer and affirmations, do so with a spirit of acceptance and expect only the best in your life.

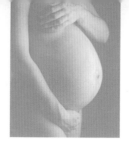

Stimulating Skin

Originating in Japan, the hot towel rub is a simple routine that rejuvenates and beautifies your skin in a short period of time. Unlike dry skin brushing or loofahs, which stimulate only the surface of the skin, the hot towel rub also works on the muscles and internal organs. It can be done on a daily basis both during and after pregnancy. While you are pregnant, it helps to prevent stretch marks and the build-up of cellulite. Afterwards, it can help to keep your skin healthy and enable it to regain its natural elasticity. It can also aid weight loss.

As well as more radiant skin, this simple routine can offer you many other benefits. It helps to increase your circulation. If you rub in the morning, you will feel refreshed and ready for the day; if you rub at night, it helps your tired muscles relax and you will find your sleep more restful and deep. It can help to strengthen your immune system and aid the smooth function of organs such as lungs, liver and kidneys.

This stimulating rub is a wonderful way to release stress and tension: it just lets the pressure out. After trying the rub for a while, you will see that it gives you as much exercise as an aerobic workout.

The hot towel rub is an inexpensive, simple and fun way to look and feel wonderful; it takes only 10–15 minutes a day. All you need is a cotton hand towel, a sink full of hot water and your bathroom.

Try this rub every morning or night (or both) before your regular bath or shower. It won't take long for you to notice the improvements in the condition of your skin – it will be smoother, firmer and more supple.

Remember to do this rub before you bathe. If you do it while you're in the bath or shower, you will lose too many minerals to the hot steam.

1 Fill your bathroom sink with hot water.

2 Dip the towel into the water, wring it out and fold it into a pad that fits comfortably in your hand.

3 Rub your entire body in a back and forth motion until your skin becomes red. The back and forth strokes should be fairly short and brisk. You do not need to rub really hard; the pressure should be firm but not painful. Be gentle with areas that are delicate or sensitive. At first, it can take a while for your skin to become red, and dryness may appear, but do not despair. Clogged fat beneath the surface of your skin prevents the natural oils from flowing smoothly. When it begins to break down, your skin will become smooth and silky to the touch.

4 Pay special attention to your feet and toes, hands and fingers, and face and neck. If you are busy, just concentrate on these areas.

By using a systematic approach to your rub, you can tailor your session to your mood. For an uplifting effect, for example, start at your feet and work up to your face, or to feel more calm, work from top to toe.

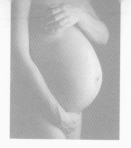

Aromatic Relaxants

Aromatherapy – 'using aromatic plants and their oils for healing' – has been used for thousands of years as a treatment to heal and soothe the whole body emotionally, physically and spiritually. Civilisations as long ago as the Egyptians in 3000BC harnessed these delightful powers.

Water is a perfect medium for using aromatherapy oils; a few drops of an essential oil in a bath, for example, can revitalise and revive or calm and sedate, depending on which oils you choose. Particular oils are helpful for alleviating aches and pains and for promoting deep, restful sleep. Simply add a few drops of the essential oil of your choice (see opposite) to warm water, relax and enjoy the benefits. In the shower, add a few drops of your chosen essential oil to a cotton washcloth and relish the delicious vapours while standing under the running water.

Massage is a great way to feel relaxed and to smooth away aching muscles. Essential oils are too potent to use directly on the skin, so first dilute a few drops of an essential oil in an almond oil base and then apply this mixture to your skin. Applying oil to your belly can help to prevent stretch marks and to maintain your skin's natural elasticity. Massage your feet, while you can, or ask your partner to take a turn or treat you with a full body massage.

oothing

Oils for Pregnancy

There are a number of oils that should be avoided during pregnancy, so check the label or ask an experienced aromatherapist for advice. Here are some oils that you might like to try. Lavender oil is very good for soothing aches and pains, especially in the legs and the back. It has stress-relieving, antidepressant and antinausea qualities and also promotes restful sleep. Mandarin is refreshing and gentle, and counters fatigue and fluid retention. Neroli is an extremely expensive oil but has the most luxurious scent. It is especially valuable for the regeneration of the skin and promotes healthy, clear skin. Tangerine is a cheerful oil that prevents stretch marks. Its mild nature helps to calm nerves with a wonderfully uplifting smell. Ylang-Ylang is an exquisite oil that is both relaxing and restoring. It is good for those who are tense or worried.

Buying and Storing Oils

When buying essential oils, choose ones in dark, glass bottles, rather than plastic bottles, and do not store oils in plastic as it degrades quickly and taints the oils. Make sure you purchase pure essential oils (only these have therapeutic properties) and buy only a small amount at one time. Expensive oils are an indication of their quality; a small amount of an expensive oil goes a long way. Store your oils in a cool, dark place.

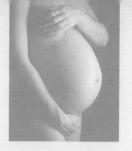

Feasting on Food

At no other time are your body and its demands changing so obviously. Respect your body: listen to it and consider how you are going to nourish and nurture the tiny baby blossoming inside you. Don't make drastic changes to your diet, instead continue to develop a healthy attitude towards food. Now is the time to focus on the quality of what you eat and to include foods that will strengthen your health and that of your baby; try out new ingredients rather than trying to deny yourself.

A home-cooked meal on a daily basis is one of the greatest gifts you can give yourself and your baby. Cooking a meal is nourishment in the purest sense and will send a direct message of love to your baby. If you sit down to eat and have your meals at the same hour each day, you will find yourself more secure, stable, balanced and satisfied.

Go Organic   Eating foods that are closest to their natural state makes us feel a connection with Mother Nature. Through them, we can develop a deep sense of belonging and feel part of the bigger picture. Eating highly processed foods or those full of chemicals creates feelings of separation: they weaken and defuse the spiritual link between you and your baby. Generally, refined foods have a desensitising and disorientating effect.

Satisfaction Energy Strength

Wondrous Wholefoods

Wholegrains contain both the seed and the fruit of a cereal. Each little grain is packed with energy and B vitamins, and provides you with strength and stamina. Eating wholegrains will help you to develop a deep sensitivity and appreciation towards all things, plus they reinforce the bond between you and your baby. Include wholegrains such as rice (in risotto), barley (in soups and stews), millet, oats (as porridge or home-made biscuits), corn and wheat (as wholewheat pasta, bulgar wheat, couscous and breads) in your meals on a daily basis.

The Pawnee Indians believed that in the beginning the great goddess Tirawa gave corn to man. The corn told man she was Mother Almighty, like Tirawa. When a grain of corn is broken, the juice within is like mother's milk. Corn was 'mother' because she nourishes. Long ago, Pawnee women did all the planting, because the Pawnee thought of all women as 'mother'; men would even call their wives 'mother' as they nourished them and gave them food.

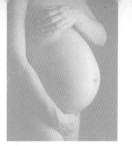

A sacred vessel ...
FEASTING ON FOOD

Your appetite may wax and wane, especially in the early months, but it usually picks up and then becomes ever-bigger. To lessen mood swings related to blood sugar highs and lows, choose sugar-free jams, juices and biscuits. Also, try natural sweeteners such as rice syrups, barley malt, fruit juice and maple syrup to keep you feeling calm and balanced.

Begin to develop a taste for fish and vegetable-quality protein such as beans, tofu, seitan and tempeh instead of meat; fish especially is rich in fatty acids vital to your baby's development. Vegetable protein is easy to absorb and assimilate. Beans and bean products are rich in essential vitamins and minerals, as well as providing slow-release energy.

Fruit &
Vegetables

Eating a wide variety of fresh fruit and vegetables will help to create a feeling of spiritual openness and a lightness of being that connects you with your baby. When selecting produce, look for foods that are grown locally and organically – farmers who love and care for the earth have grown these in harmony with the environment. By supporting their efforts, you are showing your gratitude and care for the health of the world. This subtle message of love will be absorbed by your baby and she will be born with a natural appreciation for the earth. Organically grown foods also give you stamina and vitality. Eating fresh vegetables on a daily basis helps you to feel more satisfied with your meals and they are an ideal complement to wholegrains.

Sea Vegetables

The ocean has great power; when we eat foods from the sea, we absorb that power and feel it deep inside. There are many different types of sea vegetables, each with its own unique flavour. Nori, wakame and kombu, for example, are extremely valuable as they filter important minerals – iron, calcium and zinc – into the body. They also help to discharge toxins and fat. Eating both land and sea vegetables creates a sensation of completeness, because you are connecting with your whole world.

When cooking, be sure to use unrefined oils such as olive, sesame, sunflower or safflower, which are light and easy to absorb. If you want to season food, choose unrefined sea salt over the refined table variety. Sea salt has all the trace minerals intact and is easier to absorb.

nutritious

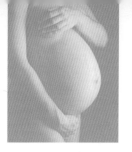

Nourishing Drinks

During pregnancy, and later on if you are breastfeeding, it is important for you to take care of yourself and make sure you are getting the nourishment your body and baby demand. What's more, nutritious milkshakes, like other naturally sweet, creamy foods, are a great way to feel more relaxed and emotionally soothed. Their calming effect on the body aids relief from the stresses of everyday life.

Oat Milk & Amazing Shake

For many centuries oats have been considered the principal grain in Ireland, Scotland, England and other parts of Europe. Known for their warming qualities, oats have a high fat and protein content and are also rich in B vitamins and the minerals iron and calcium. Their creamy texture and rich taste make a fantastic base for this energy-rich shake. You may prefer to prepare the *Oat Milk* a few days in advance and store it in the fridge until you want to flavour it.

Rice syrup has a texture similar to honey with a lovely mild flavour. It is made from a mixture of rice and sprouted rice or barley, which is then fermented. This gentle sweetener contains complex sugars that are digested slowly and enter the bloodstream in a steady manner, thus helping to maintain the body's blood sugar levels. Rice

For the milk

450ml fruit juice or spring water
A pinch of sea salt
25g rolled oats
3 tablespoons rice syrup

1 Place the juice or water and sea salt in a pan, bring to the boil on a medium flame.

2 Lightly whisk in the rolled oats.

3 Cover with a lid and simmer for about 15–20 minutes.

4 Blend the oat mixture and rice syrup together while still hot.

5 Allow to cool before making the shake.

Oat Milk

For the shake

450ml apple-strawberry juice
225ml vanilla soya milk or 2 tablespoons tahini
450ml oat milk
1–2 tablespoons rice syrup
625g strawberries, rinsed and halved (keep a few back and slice finely for a garnish)

1 Place all the ingredients in a blender.

2 Blend for about 2–3 minutes to create a smooth, creamy drink.

3 Serve lightly chilled in tall glasses and garnish with the finely sliced strawberries.

This recipe makes enough for 4-6 people.

If you wish to make a thicker shake, reduce the amount of juice you use. Experiment with other fruits such as peaches, apricots, apples, raspberries, lemons or even orange rind.

For a milder or sweeter taste, reduce or increase the amount of rice syrup you add to the mixture.

You could add a pinch of cinnamon for a spicier shake.

Amazing Shake

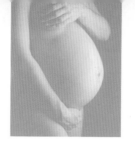

syrup gives you enduring energy without the highs and lows of other stronger sweets. When you fancy something sweet, use this syrup – it can be used to sweeten teas, desserts or even as a spread on bread.

Make this deliciously simple, smooth, creamy shake using your *Oat Milk* and the finest organic ingredients; the recipe is outlined on the previous page. A quick pick-me-up, *Amazing Shake* is easy to prepare and is substantial enough to be a small meal in itself. This shake is a lovely, comforting drink that you can also enjoy with your friends.

Sweet Vegetable Tea

This delightful tea has a delicate, sweet taste. It is made from fresh vegetables that are finely sliced, cooked for 20 minutes and then removed so that their essences and flavours remain. *Sweet Vegetable Tea* is the perfect drink to have on a regular basis. During pregnancy, it helps your muscles to relax, lets anxiety melt away and leaves you feeling calm and at ease. Drink this tea for a few days to experience a wondrous opening-up sensation, as if any internal pressure you have is released and your energy is able to flow smoothly. It is also extremely beneficial for balancing blood sugar levels.

The tea's mild sweetness gives you stable, slow-release energy that creates vitality for you to enjoy your day. This gentle drink is great for breastfeeding because it aids milk production. Drink this tea at least three times a week to receive the full benefits. You'll feel its relaxing properties best if you make it fresh on the day you wish to drink it.

For the tea

675ml spring water
Half an onion, finely sliced
Half a carrot, washed and finely sliced
A handful of cabbage, washed and shredded
2.5cm slice of hard green winter squash,
    washed, seeds removed and finely sliced

1 Put the water in a pan and bring to the boil on a medium flame.

2 Add all the vegetables and simmer uncovered for about 2 minutes.

3 Cover and simmer on a low flame for 15–20 minutes.

4 Remove the vegetables immediately and drink while hot.

If you cannot get hold of the squash, use a little extra of the other vegetables to make up the weight.

If you want to drink the tea during the day, it can easily be decanted into a thermos.

Sweet Vegetable Tea

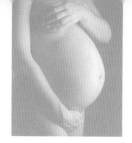

Remedies for Mothers

The combination of aches, pains, nausea and exhaustion sometimes experienced during pregnancy may leave you feeling depleted and low. Don't let these negative symptoms depress you. Instead, put yourself in touch with the incredible processes that are going on within you and turn to a natural remedy to ease the strain.

Many expectant mothers experience some morning sickness, nausea and vomiting – a miserable but natural part of pregnancy. Sipping juice, eating small, frequent meals and also taking gentle exercise can help to ease the nausea. Many mothers also swear by natural remedies. Ginger, for example, has long been used as a remedy for sickness of all kinds and it's available in many forms; steep some freshly grated root ginger in hot water for a settling tea. In addition, infusions of camomile, hops, peppermint, lemon balm, meadowsweet, blackhorehound, gentian and raspberry leaf all help to settle the stomach. Aromatherapy can help – lavender, camomile and rose oils are especially good.

Morning sickness can strike at any time, provoked by the most diverse of stimuli. Try to pinpoint what triggers your own nausea and then take steps to avoid such prompts. You could use flowers, for example, or fruits such as lemons, to override stomach-turning smells.

Backache is also a common problem for pregnant women. As you will be carrying a lot of weight at the front of your body, you may thrust your shoulders back and your stomach forwards in order to maintain your balance. This puts a lot of strain on your spine and will cause discomfort unless you have a strong back. Swimming and yoga are excellent for back strengthening, thus alleviating any pain and making you more mobile. Improving your posture is crucial – flatten the curve of your back and try bending your knees a little. Homeopathic help is also at hand: if your spine or hips feel weak, take *Aesculus*; if you feel burning in the spine and the small of your back feels weak, try *Kali carb*.

Tiredness is part and parcel of being pregnant. In the first few months, much of a mother's resources are channelled into forming the placenta. In later pregnancy, insomnia is very common, as it can be hard to get comfortable in bed; you may also have to make frequent visits to the toilet and baby can get very frisky. If you cannot get comfortable, try surrounding yourself with pillows. If you want to sleep on your stomach, then use pillows to make a 'cave' for the bulge. And if indigestion or breathlessness keep you awake at night, try sleeping propped up, with pillows on all sides and under your knees.

Camomile

Gentian

Peppermint

A mother is a mother still,
The holiest thing alive.

Homeopathic remedies can help at night; try *Cocculus* or *Coffea crud* when you cannot sleep. Herbal infusions made with hops, passion flower, elderflower, Californian poppy or valerian can also encourage valuable sleep. You could even use these herbs in a hot bath. Simply pour boiling water into a large bowl with one or two handfuls of the herb and leave it for an hour, then strain it and pour into your bath.

Practise relaxation techniques before retiring to bed. Soothing classical music relaxes both baby and you, while rock music may cause her to kick and become restless. Reflexology can promote tranquility throughout your body while massage can help to ease you into a deep, revitalising sleep. Try putting a drop of neroli oil or clary sage on the edge of your pillow, or using a few drops in your base massage oil.

The best remedy for fatigue is more sleep – don't fight it. Sleep holds the key to recharging your energy and spirit the natural way. When this option is unavailable, cut down on your activity levels and take frequent rests. Above all, treat yourself indulgently. Give yourself permission to go to bed whenever you feel particularly tired and become a willing recipient of all the love and assistance that is offered to you.

Crystal Power

Each gemstone or crystal has a great history due to its time spent deep within the earth. Crystals have long been recognised for their healing properties by traditional cultures throughout the world, but these powers should be harnessed wisely and not be over used.

Crystals act like 'little generators' that can charge the energy of you, your baby, your home and those who live in it. When purchasing crystals, choose one that appeals to you and exudes a happy feeling. A simple blessing and giving thanks to the earth will help to recharge the positive energy that your crystal provides.

During pregnancy, use crystals to enhance positive emotions and to help you feel more calm and relaxed. There are many different crystals to choose from, each with its own unique power.

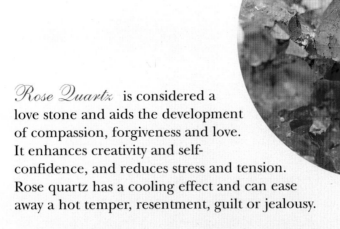

Rose Quartz is considered a love stone and aids the development of compassion, forgiveness and love. It enhances creativity and self-confidence, and reduces stress and tension. Rose quartz has a cooling effect and can ease away a hot temper, resentment, guilt or jealousy.

Amethyst is found in a spectrum of purples, from a lovely pale lavender to deep violet. Considered a very enchanting and powerful stone for spiritual awareness, amethyst can be used in meditation and to aid creative thinking. This romantic stone imparts heightened intuition, inspiration and divine love. An amethyst placed under your pillow can dispel any difficulties you may have sleeping.

Haematite is a dense mineral with a rich metallic lustre and steel-grey colour. This gemstone is extremely 'grounding'. It boosts concentration, original thinking and all types of detailed work. Haematite also has energising and vitalising properties and enhances personal magnetism, willpower and courage. You need to feel attracted to it to receive the full benefits. This stone is effective during pregnancy as it slowly strengthens the body and lifts negativity and depression. During childbirth it is said to prevent excessive bleeding.

PROTECTIVE DEVICES ...
CRYSTAL POWER

Green Jade gives off an aura of tranquillity and peacefulness. It radiates divine unconditional love and helps you to feel emotionally balanced. Jade helps you feel more grounded and capable of dealing with any situation that life throws at you.

Amber is the fossilised resin of prehistoric pine trees. It radiates a wonderful solidified golden light, which is healing, soothing and harmonising. Carry a stone with you, in a pocket for example, to help to clear your mind and enhance your ability to concentrate.

Tiger's Eye helps to connect you with your personal power. It can soften stubbornness and give you a feeling of determination rather than obstinacy. Tiger's eye has a balancing energy – it is very grounding and centring. If you sleep with a stone under your pillow throughout your pregnancy, it will encourage a safe labour; if held during labour itself, it gives you the strength you need.

Jasper is a very grounding stone and a powerful healer. It helps you to feel calm and able to handle difficulties with a clear head. Jasper stabilises your energy and brings you into the centre, away from feeling too frantic on the one hand or unmotivated on the other. If you have disturbed sleep or nightmares, jasper can be placed underneath your bed pillow for deeper, more restful nights.

Turquoise can tone and strengthen the body. It centres your being on love and a feeling of being connected to others. Turquoise draws you into unconditional love for all people and brings with it peace of mind, loyalty and friendship.

Pale-green Soapstone is beautiful to behold and wonderful for inner strength and healing. It balances the female reproductive organs and promotes a healthy pregnancy. Soapstone also helps to align mother and baby, strengthening this very special bond.

In addition to individual raw crystal specimens, crystals can be worn as jewellery, as large amber pendants or a tiger's eye ring for example, or bought as sculptured shapes such as a rose quartz heart or a green jade animal. The important thing is to choose one that appeals to you and that you feel has the energy that enhances your spirit.

Natural crystals need to be cleaned occasionally to recharge their energy. You could either place them on a cloth made from natural fibres, such as cotton or silk, and leave them in the sun for three to four hours or soak them in warm salted water for at least 24 hours.

Glass crystals can also be used to bring energy into your home. Hung in a window to catch the sunlight, they radiate a rainbow of colours throughout the room. Choose ones that are regular in shape; crystals that are jagged can create a more chaotic atmosphere.

Power Incense

The sensual smell of incense conjures up visions of the mystic, religious ceremonies and of wandering through Middle Eastern bazaars. Incense has been used for thousands of years and was considered to be incredibly valuable: some types were worth as much as gold. Incense doesn't actually burn, rather it smoulders and, in a similar way to lighting a candle, its essence disappears into the atmosphere. Churches, temples and monasteries use incense to clear stagnated energy and create an atmosphere suited to prayer and meditation.

Using Pot-pourri

Like some pregnant women, you may find the fragrance of incense too heady and strong. A milder way to give your home a marvellous scent, and also to make you feel comforted and at peace, is to use pot-pourri. Choose naturally scented pot-pourri, based on essential oils. You can display pot-pourri in lovely bowls or baskets and, when their smell fades, refresh them with drops of the appropriate oil. Or make fragrant sachets by placing a small amount of pot-pourri in the centre of a fabric square, gather up the sides and tie a ribbon around the top. Using fragrance gives your home that unique and special feeling; a simple way to create a loving and safe space for you to enjoy your pregnancy.

Burning incense in your home purifies and charges the existing energy. The gently smouldering fragrance will drift throughout your house to create a relaxing and inspiring feeling.

Incense is made up of a combination of resins, gums, spices and herbs that can be burnt to give a delightful fragrance. What smells good is very personal. Some fragrances are relaxing while others stimulate the senses. It is important to choose one that suits how your feel.

Quality is key when buying incense. Modern incense comes in the form of sticks, cones and preprepared mixes that are burnt on charcoal discs. The stick form is the most popular because it is easy to use.

Different aromas are available to suit you and your mood; it is a good idea to try them out before deciding which ones are right for you.

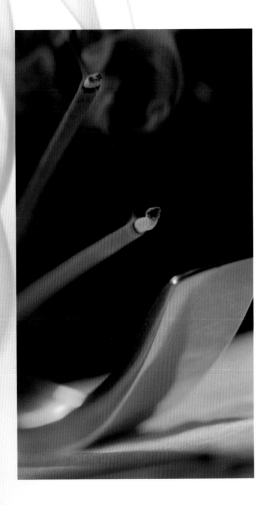

Sandalwood can soothe, release fear, reduce stress and create a sensual, relaxed environment.

Frankincense has been used in almost all Middle Eastern religions as a sacred gift to the gods. It is calming and helps to release fear.

Myrrh is available in sweet and bitter varieties and is used to create strength and inspiration. Sweet Myrrh is smouldered to evoke feelings of love.

You can also carry the scented stick and cleanse a particular room by waving it softly into corners and around the centre. A simple prayer said at the same time will enhance this energising and protective process.

Powerful Creatures

Many traditional and tribal cultures have a high regard for animals and the spirits that are expressed within them. They believe every animal has special powers and wisdom by virtue of its being part of nature. The unique power in each species of animal can guide, teach and protect.

In China, the tiger, dragon, tortoise and phoenix are considered auspicious animals and bring good fortune. The tiger has the ability to defend and can detect the presence of any danger. The dragon symbolises the wisdom of the mind, the future and spirituality. The tortoise provides great security and longevity, while the mythical phoenix represents inspiration, beauty and a capacity for vision.

Native American children at around the age of puberty were sent out on a vision quest to find their power animal. This animal would give them confidence and status among their tribe and would also protect, give power and assistance to the growing child. The Celts also honoured animals, and the Druids could speak the magic language of birds.

During your pregnancy, reflect on which animal you feel is right to protect and watch over your baby. Each animal has its own qualities, so select one you feel represents something special to you and your baby. Butterflies, for example, represent delicacy, freedom and lightness. Bears are sacred animals and have great power and endurance. Deer are appreciated for their beauty and gentleness. The panda brings gentle strength, nourishment and sensitivity, while the zebra shows that agility, not strength, brings success and encourages individuality.

The animal could be in one or many forms: a wooden, clay or china figurine or, perhaps, a pictorial representation. Keep in mind that any power creature should look friendly and not frighten a child. To enhance your baby's character, you may want to investigate your baby's Chinese astrological animal, like monkey or horse, based on the year she was born (see pages 114–19).

Good Luck Charms

The magical powers of charms, amulets and talismans have been used the world over to protect against the Evil Eye. Selecting a good luck charm for you or your baby adds a magical touch that makes your birth experience enchanting. Browse in antique markets or speciality shops for items that are unique; small figurines, carved stone animals, charms that have been used in times past or even a beautiful shawl with a fringed edge. When choosing your baby's charm, make sure that it will be safe for her. If you want to pass on a piece of jewellery with significant meaning, then you may want to keep it in a pretty box until your baby is older. Avoid anything that she can put in her mouth or choke on. To cleanse away any old vibrations, wash the charm in salted water and make it truly yours. Place the charm in a special place to watch over and protect you and your baby during her growing years.

The use of charms dates as far back as the Old Testament, in which they are mentioned in the book of Genesis. Jewish people wear charms and hand-shaped amulets known as Hamsas for protection against disease, physical injury and the Evil Eye. The Blue Eye, another protective charm, is used among Jewish and Greek people.

Simple charms have been used in many cultures to protect the newborn babe. In Russia, a red ribbon was tied around the baby's wrist for good luck, while a small piece of bread and a little bag of salt were tied together, again with red ribbon, and placed in the cot. Sometimes, a red ribbon would be threaded around the cot for extra protection.

In many Latin countries, small protective charms were pinned to the baby's undergarments. Little bracelets were also placed on the baby's wrist and charms were added over the years.

Believed to have magical powers and send out positive vibrations, amulets protect you against evil and are usually worn or carried upon a person. Amulets come in many forms, such as crystals, unique symbols, astrological signs or messages. In medieval Europe, women wore rings with inscriptions and particular crystals or gemstones on different fingers at different times of the year.

In the Middle East, silver bracelets and anklets with bells as well as fringed and tasselled garments were used to ward off bad spirits. In India, silver filigree necklaces and rings were worn to help keep away evil; in Africa, bones and cowrie shells were used in everyday jewellery and charms for their protective powers. Some of these protective practices are still carried out today.

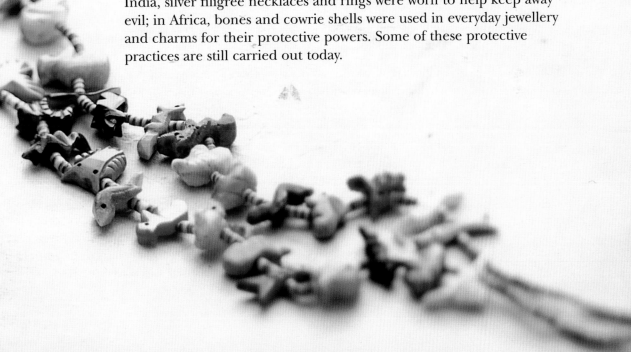

Space Cleansing

The nesting sensation that many women feel towards the end of their pregnancies is a natural urge to create a beautiful space in which to begin family life. This sensation most resembles spring cleaning, a concept that has existed for hundreds of years. In earlier times, the cleansing ritual lasted a week and was carried out twice a year, once in the spring and again in the fall. Everything down to the very last detail was washed, cleaned, put out in the sun, beaten or scrubbed. The incredible love and effort that went into cleaning resulted in a fresh, sparkling, clean and healthy home – the kind you want to bring your baby home to. The deeper your cleaning, the better the results. Wash the windows; clean in all the corners and cupboards; dust the furniture; wipe down all the surfaces; clean the curtains and linen; and vacuum the carpets. Air rugs and bedding outside in the sun; sunlight has a cleansing and refreshing energy.

Deep cleansing can also change the vibration in your living space. Energy stagnates over time, especially around clutter or in a corner, and creates a heavy feeling; it can make it difficult for you to be active, positive and happy. In preparation for your baby, recharge the energy in your home through cleansing and rituals that will strongly affect the way you act and feel.

Make space for your baby to come into your life. Clear out the clutter. Go through your belongings and get rid of any that you don't feel are useful or believe to be beautiful. When you get something new, give something away. Before cleansing your home, you may like to perform a simple meditation to calm your mind and help you create a positive image. Find somewhere quiet and comfortable to sit. Breathe slowly and deeply for a few minutes, and then visualise your home bright and sparkling, each room clean and clear.

Salt

Sea salt has the power to charge your own energy and that of your surroundings. It has a very strong, cleansing effect and can create a stable feeling. After cleaning your home or a room, sprinkle sea salt in the corners or any place that feels blocked or heavy. For a fast and efficient cleansing, you can toss sea salt around you in a clockwise direction, using a wide sweeping motion with your arms. Leave the sea salt where it falls for a few hours to absorb any negative energy in the room, and then vacuum it up.

To create more stability in your home, fill small bowls with sea salt and place them in the north-east and south-west corners of your home. If you have small children put the bowls on a shelf so they will be out of reach. Replace the sea salt every month.

Water

Use the purifying properties of water to create a feeling of harmony and peace. Small, indoor waterfalls have a lovely, healing sound that creates an uplifting feeling in a room, while aquaria add peace and tranquillity. Living plants and fish create a restful, soothing energy. If you do not have enough space for these water features, 'solar-charge' some water by placing a bowl of water outside in the sun or by a sunny window for three hours. Solar-charged water creates a cheerful energy, particularly in a room that is dark and heavy. Put the charged water in the room you wish to revitalise and leave it for a day. Replace the water each morning.

Preparing the nest ...
SPACE CLEANSING

Sound The use of sound in cleansing carries a very powerful vibration and has the ability to change the energy in a room quickly. Clapping is very effective for dispersing energy. Walk slowly around the room and clap in the corners. In areas where the energy is bright, your claps will resonate crisp and strong, whereas in stale areas, your claps will have a muffled sound. Clap starting at the floor, working up the walls toward the ceiling to disperse stagnant energy. Singing songs that make you feel happy and playing music will energise your home. The laughter of children helps to give your home a joyful and positive feeling.

Candles Ideal in rooms that feel dark and damp, candles help to uplift the spirit and make you feel more positive and aware. White candles are the most suitable colour for meditation purposes. Pale-green candles represent new beginnings and are perfect for ceremonies connected to the birth of your baby. Place them in areas where the family spends time together. Generally, green candles enhance feelings of peace and growth.

Aromatics Roses, lavender, lemon verbena or a sprig of pine can be used for cleansing, too. Use a bowl of solar-charged water. Give the water your blessing and thank it for bringing new life and light into your space. Dip the flower or plant of your choice into the water and lightly flick the water around the room starting in the eastern corner and moving in a clockwise direction. Pay particular attention to the corners of the room. This cleansing ceremony results in a beautiful, airy atmosphere.

Sandalwood is especially good for providing protection and creating positive feelings. In incense form, it will fill your home with a wonderful fragrance. Cinnamon increases feelings of happiness. Place a stick of cinnamon in a pan of water or apple juice. Put the pan on a low heat and allow the deliciously spiced scent to waft through the house.

Using Feng Shui

Imagine for a moment you are walking into a nursery. The walls are painted a soft pastel shade and happy pictures add a sparkle of interest. Immediately you feel more calm and reassured. The furnishings are made from natural materials and the room is reminiscent of a perfect spring day, uplifting and refreshing. Toys are neatly stored in boxes and on shelves and a mobile gently sways back and forth. Bright, leafy green plants hang in the windows and a rocking chair invites to you to rest and dream a while. An atmosphere of new beginnings flows all around and it seems like the perfect place for your baby to sleep and play. This is the art of Feng Shui softly at work for you.

Feng Shui has been practised for many thousands of years in the East and is now becoming very popular in the West. Literally translated as 'Wind and Water', Feng Shui looks at ways in which you can become one with your environment and use the positive energy that exists within and around your living space. You do not have to be an expert to experience the benefits of Feng Shui. Even a few simple changes can improve any space and bring you great rewards.

Once your baby is born, the nursery is the place where you and she will spend a lot of time. The room needs to be uplifting and stimulating when your baby is awake, while maintaining a sense of calm and quiet when she rests. At night, daily nourishment is absorbed throughout the baby's body and it is the time when she grows the most. Untroubled sleep is vital for her development.

The colours, style and placement of furniture and decorations will have a direct effect on how your baby feels. When choosing your décor, take time to consider some of these simple Feng Shui ideas and give your baby a special gift that will last throughout her early years.

The Use of Colour and Pattern

aColours affect how we feel and they set the mood for a room. Pale yellow is a balanced shade and is good to use as a base for any nursery. Pastel shades have a soft effect whereas 'true' blues and greens have more of a cooling influence. Strong colours – red, orange, purple and bright yellow – are highly stimulating and are better suited as accents for the room. Once your baby is born, soft pastel colours will help her if she has trouble sleeping, but if you find that she is timid and overly quiet, add more strongly coloured paintings and accessories to help lift her spirit and provide uplifting energy.

If you wish to use a pattern on the walls, be sure to choose a soft, subtle design. Overly busy wallpaper and wallcoverings create chaotic energy, which could overstimulate an active baby. Plain painted walls help to create an orderly atmosphere, but if you want to give them a lift, then stencils are a fun way to add interest. Use them around the top of walls or at random in the room. Hang happy, cheerful paintings and later, when the baby grows, use some of her own art to strengthen her identity and recapture memories of trips, holidays or special occasions.

Preparing the nest ...

USING FENG SHUI

Natural Materials

Wood, one of the five elements in Feng Shui, has a neutral energy. When selecting furniture, choose items made from solid wood. These will create an airy atmosphere in the room, especially if you choose light-coloured wood such as pine or painted pieces in pale colours.

A wooden cot with a solid headboard encourages a feeling of stability and security for the baby. Furniture with rounded edges creates a softer atmosphere and energy will flow naturally throughout the room; furniture with sharp edges is not as safe for the baby as she grows. Avoid overfilling the nursery with furniture or using pieces that are dark and heavy. Aim to create a room that feels spacious and open.

When choosing bedding, sheets, curtains and rugs for your nursery, look for ones made from natural fibres such as cotton, linen, silk or wool. Synthetic fabrics carry a static electric charge that creates an imbalanced feeling and a chaotic energy in the room. Natural fabrics help to buffer the effects of the electromagnetic influences that are present in all homes today. Cotton-filled futons are available in cot size, and flannel sheets make for restful sleep. Cotton quilts attract less dust and produce a refreshing vibration. Wooden floors with area rugs made from wool or cotton prevent stagnation and are easy to clean. If you want wall-to-wall carpet, choose one made from pure wool.

They say there is no other,
Can take the place of mother.

Toys

Natural fabrics such as cotton, silk or wool create a soft, peaceful type of energy. Soft toys made from these fabrics help to make a baby feel safe and secure. The fresh, bright energy of a room is lost when lots of toys are left lying about: energy stagnates around clutter, thus breaking the natural flow. Plan the nursery so that when your baby is older, toys can be stored easily in wicker baskets on shelves, in cupboards or in boxes.

Mobiles are both quietly stimulating and relaxing to a baby. Brightly coloured or shiny mobiles create more excitement, while pastel, fabric ones are more peaceful. Hang mobiles in a place that is easy for your baby to see but not directly over her cot. The graceful movement of mobiles causes energy to flow in a slow, steady manner.

Space Planning

Maintain an open and spacious feeling in the room by positioning the furniture carefully; don't, for example, let pieces jut out into the room or obstruct windows. Position a rocking chair so that, when seated, you have an open view of the whole room and door. Place the cot against a wall with open space around it to ensure a good night's sleep for your baby. Make sure there is nothing hanging over the bed, like a shelf or cupboard, as this will create a feeling of pressure and causes uneasy, restless sleep. If the nursery has a sloping or pointed ceiling, do not position the cot beneath it as it will be surrounded by highly active energy, not ideal for deep sleep. Avoid placing a cot beneath a window or directly opposite the door. The lively energy coming through these openings will make it difficult for her to calm down enough to sleep.

Peaceful

Green Leafy Plants

Plants are ideal for bringing fresh energy into the nursery and they clean and refresh the air, too. Plants have the ability to absorb noise and make us feel relaxed and calm. Spider plants, golden pothos and elephant-eared philodendron are the most efficient cleaners. These are common house plants and are easy to care for. Large, round-leafed plants have quiet energy, and cascading plants create calmness. Avoid spiky plants or cacti in your baby's room as they give off active, cutting energy. Place plants away from little hands on high shelves or hang them in front of windows. Lavish loving care on your plants to maximise their positive energy; wilted plants have negative energy.

Using the energy created by living plants and natural furnishings will help to combat the effects of any electromagnetic radiation from electrical appliances. This radiation has a direct effect on health, and babies and young children are particularly sensitive. It is a good idea to keep electrical gadgets to a minimum in the nursery.

Natural Airy Spacious

Lighting

A nursery filled with natural light has a positive, uplifting energy, especially if the room gets the morning sun. If natural light is in short supply, paint the walls a light colour to reflect the available light and use uplighters on the walls to help create an airy atmosphere. Avoid table and floor lamps so that later on when your baby is up and about, she will not be tempted to experiment with plug sockets and electrical wires. Keep curtains or blinds open during the day so that the room enjoys the maximum of fresh and bright outside energy.

Night-time

To establish a calm, peaceful environment at night, keep all doors shut and curtains or blinds closed. If the bedroom door faces a staircase or bathroom, your baby could become anxious and difficult, so hang a small wind chime above the door to dispel worrying energy. If you want soft lighting, use a tea-light candle in a holder or a small lantern. Place well away from the cot and extinguish it before going to bed.

Creating a Small Space

If you live in a small flat and cannot provide a separate nursery room for your baby, do not worry. You can create a loving space in your own bedroom or living room, using a moveable screen or bookcase to create a clear partition. Apply the above mentioned ideas and incorporate as many as you can in this specially created space to give your baby a beautiful area in which to sleep, play and develop in a positive manner.

Good Wishes Blanket

During your pregnancy, it is a good idea to partake in many activities that are peaceful and prepare you for the birth of your child. Pastimes that include sewing, knitting, reading, painting, writing, gardening and listening to music are calming pursuits and will help your baby to receive positive vibrations and so feel safe and protected.

Today, we are often exposed to negative vibrations that diffuse our ability to connect to a higher power that nourishes and lightens our spirit. The presence of violence in society on all levels and the dominance of television foster feelings of fear and a negative outlook on life. In order to send a message of love and safety to your growing infant, refrain from watching any violent or horror programmes or reading disturbing material.

Creative activities not only help you to feel calm and happy but also make you feel nourished and satisfied. A good wishes baby blanket is an enchanting way to put your love into a gift for your new baby – a gift that will become a family heirloom. There are many different types of baby blanket; read through the different examples here and choose one that appeals to your senses and taste.

Baby blankets are easy to make because at their simplest they are just large rectangles of fabric. Have fun and browse through material shops and haberdashery departments to find materials that you love and that mean something to you. Look for vintage fabrics at jumble sales, flea markets and antique shows. Their bold colours and imaginative patterns make for great blankets. Choose fabrics that feel soft and luxurious; use an embroidered organza and back it with a matching shade of taffeta or try velvet backed with patterned wool in a similar colour. Colour-wise, anything goes: pick pastel colours such as soft pinks, lilacs, lemon, quiet blues and cooling greens or go for a contrast with navy blue offset with a white backing. These gorgeous blankets can be used as a cover for your baby or as a lap rug for you to enjoy. Use blankets as throws to soften and bring life to the nursery, too.

Baby sleeping bags are also simple to make. Pick pure cotton flannel and use cotton batting for a filler. Sewing patterns for these are readily available in most material shops. Sleeping bags are practical for travelling or for keeping your baby warm outside of the nursery. If you are away from home they transform into simple bedding and can be unzipped to create a practical changing mat.

PREPARING THE NEST ...
GOOD WISHES BLANKET

Baby blankets can be knitted in lovely colours and patterns. Knitting was believed to have started when primitive humans first made webs out of roots and tendrils. There is evidence of knitting in Peru as far back as 100BC and other examples have been found in Egypt, Saudi Arabia and Europe from around the fourth and fifth centuries. Knitting is a very relaxing pastime and helps to reduce stress. Even a beginner can tackle a baby blanket because the straightforward shape can easily be knitted on large needles. Select pure wool because it will have a neutral effect on your baby. Synthetic wool carries a strong static charge and can create an imbalance in the body's energies. Finish your wool blanket with a 'good luck' fringe or edge it with satin.

Quilting also has a long and rich history. One of the earliest examples may have been in Egypt in 3400BC. In the Middle Ages and the Renaissance period, quilting became a decorative art as well as a way to keep warm. In Eastern cultures, quilted garments were used as a form of armour. Patchwork quilts were created from scraps of fabric saved from dressmaking. In colonial America, every scrap of material was valuable and was saved to patch and repair clothing and bedding. Beautiful needlework and embroidery were used to create the patchwork effect. Crazy quilting was a popular Victorian pastime. Pieces of fancy fabric in different shapes were sewn together with no planned design. Patchwork quilts can be easy or extremely detailed and they make fantastic baby blankets. Collect pieces of material from clothes that have specific memories for you or buy small swatches from fabric stores. Cut the fabric into squares or hexagonal shapes. Then sew them together by hand for an antique effect. Continue patchworking until you have a large enough rectangle for your baby blanket. Use a solid colour to edge around the quilt. Quilting is a wonderful activity that the whole family can do together. Your patchwork quilt makes for exciting stories about magic bedspreads. Children love listening to make-believe stories, especially if they are included as characters in them.

To add a personal and elegant touch, you can monogram your baby blanket – by hand or by machine. You can use your baby's initials or a family name to create a unique blanket. The love and effort you lavish onto your piece of art can be enjoyed by future generations.

Sweetes' li'l feller,
Everybody knows;
Dunno what to call 'im,
But his mighty lak' a rose!

Sacred Spaces

We naturally create special or sacred spaces for ourselves, be they a quiet seat in a garden, a collection of photos on a dresser or a shelf with objects that have a special meaning to us alone. A sacred space provides an opportunity to feel blessed and at peace. It can signify our respect and gratitude for loved ones or evoke charming memories. Creating a sacred space or a baby blessing altar is a simple and exquisite way to honour and spiritually connect with the arrival of new life.

In the nursery, a modest arrangement of soft animals, dolls, books and wooden toys can become a sacred space. Arrange them so that your baby will be able to see them from his cot. The familiarity and comfort he will receive from seeing the arrangement every day will help to make him feel secure, soothed and calm.

A Baby Blessing Altar

The powerful effect of a sacred space can be enhanced in the form of an altar. Traditional symbols for protection and good luck can be added to bless the baby and to celebrate his journey through life. A tabletop, a windowsill, an interesting wicker knick-knack shelf or even a little wooden crate can be used as a base for your altar. Arrange it in a place where it will be, for a while at least, out of the reach of little hands.

56

In preparation for the placement of objects, the space needs to be cleansed: use warm salted water and wash the area well; for other space-cleansing techniques turn to pages 42–45. Always keep the altar clean and free from dust. Bless the area and ask for protection for your baby. Give thanks for all the good things that will be in your baby's life.

Practical Ideas

Here are some suggestions for setting up your own baby blessing altar. Use your imagination to make something that is charming and unique for you and your baby. Develop your own ideas or pick from some of the following. The altar can be very simple with only a few objects or more elaborate, depending on your taste and creativity.

Fabric makes an enchanting backdrop for your altar. Drape a delicate silk scarf over a wooden shelf for a graceful look or select pieces of fabric in colours and textures that depict new life and new beginnings, such as fine velvet or finely woven materials in creams and pastels.

Crystals will add an uplifting, re-energising aspect. Rose quartz is ideal because it fosters love, children and family. Jade is another lovely gemstone that encourages abundance and unconditional love. One of each is enough; you do not want to overdo it.

Tea-lights set in pink or white holders can be simply decorated with golden moons, stars or suns. A pink holder represents love, playfulness and youth while a white one denotes purity and innocence.

Toys such as soft, white animals represent the newborn and his character. Choose toys that are beautiful and have a lovable or peaceful feeling. If you want to bring a sense of fun and lightness to your baby's blessing altar, add a humorous toy.

Statues of saints or angels are symbols of protection for the baby. If you prefer, you could include instead a personal good luck charm.

Plants that are healthy and green represent the wellbeing of your baby, plus they offer bright, fresh energy to the nursery. Make sure you look after any plants so that they can grow along with your baby.

Think of your altar both as something that will change and grow along with your baby and as a light, loving, fun way to connect with his spirit. As he develops, add personal aspects to represent his life: a lock of hair, first-drawn pictures or small artefacts collected from walks. Photographs of him along with those of other family members could form a central focus or you might like to frame some poems or personal blessings.

Celebratory Candles

Candlelight creates a warm, glowing, enchanted atmosphere. Lit or unlit, candles add charm to many occasions and they make a perfect gift for your new baby on his arrival. Candles do not need to be saved for special occasions, their beauty and elegance can be enjoyed daily.

A New Beginnings Candle

To express some of the love you feel for your new baby, make her a gift of a special candle. Use your imagination to create something personal and let it fill your home with the wonder of natural illumination. A simple white candle in a white holder with white ribbon and fresh white flowers, for example, can represent the purity of new life and can be a thing of beauty in the soon-to-be-occupied nursery. Or try green candles in white holders with white ribbon and flowers for a cooler effect. A blue candle in a painted blue holder decorated with dried lavender and a blue checked ribbon contributes to a country feeling, while pink candles placed in frosted glass holders give off an atmosphere of love.

You don't have to mould the candle from scratch; you can easily decorate an existing candle or use wax crystals, which are easy to find in craft shops. Use them to fill shells, old tins or decorated plant pots. All you need to do is add a wick and you've created an instant candle.

For the candle

500ml water
Saucepan
Church candle
Folded tea-towel
Small silk flowers and leaves
Star-shaped confetti
Small dish
Metal spoon
Gold-leafing kit, which includes glue
Thin satin ribbon
Saucer

1 Bring half a litre of water to a boil in a saucepan. Meanwhile, place the candle on a folded tea-towel and the silk flowers, leaves and stars in a small dish.

2 Dip the spoon into the water for about 4–5 seconds. Then, rub the spoon over a section of the candle to soften the wax.

3 Press a leaf into the softened candle and press it firmly with your fingers. Reheat the spoon in the boiling water, and rub it over the leaf to seal it in place.

4 Repeat with the flowers and stars to create a pattern over your candle.

5 Spread a small amount of gold-leafing glue around the top of the candle, and wait until it becomes transparent.

6 Place a piece of gold-leaf paper over the glue. The dull side should face downwards onto the candle. Rub the paper with your fingers and simply remove the paper. The gold leaf creates a unique pattern. Use the gold leafing on other parts of the candle if you wish to make your own special design.

7 Wrap the ribbon around the candle and secure at the bottom with a bow. Then, place the candle in a saucer and surround it with silk flowers. For a more vibrant effect, use fresh flowerheads from the garden.

New Beginnings Candle

Candle Holders

Even a simple candle looks special and unique when placed in an appropriate holder. Odd pieces of fine china, such as cups and saucers, plates, jugs and sugar bowls, make elegant candle holders and can be found in jumble sales and flea markets. Garden centres often feature animal holders such as those with rabbits or frogs and you can wind ivy around the bottom of the holder to continue the natural theme. Inexpensive embossed glass tumblers make attractive sparkling surrounds for small, flickering tea-lights.

For an enchanting home-made arrangement, paint or spray a number of walnut shells gold. Place a small amount of plasticine in the bottom of each shell and secure a cake candle to serve as a mast. Fill a large glass bowl with water, add some flower petals from the garden and gently place the walnut 'boats' in the water, light the candles and watch the magical trail of lights go sailing among the flowers.

A new baby is like the beginning of things – wonder, hope, a dream of possibilities.

A Candle for All Seasons

An idea to incorporate candles in a display and to bring some natural outdoor beauty into your home is to create an arrangement to reflect, say, the season in which your baby will be born. For a spring child, fill terracotta pots with wax crystals and surround with pots of narcissi and primroses, add moss and cute little chicks. If yours is to be a summer child, arrange a profusion of vividly coloured flowers or soft pink roses encircling gold candles in gold-painted holders. For an autumn baby, use tiny pumpkins and gem squash as unique candle holders and decorate them with richly coloured red, gold and yellow leaves. White lace, frosted glass holders, berries and silver or gold candles create an imaginative display for a winter baby.

Couvade

Though the modern Western father is encouraged to be involved with all aspects of pregnancy and birth, it is a rare man who exhibits actual physical symptoms of pregnancy, such as nausea, food cravings or abdominal swellings. In many small-scale societies, however, men will mimic the experiences of women; known as couvade, this practice extends across regions of Africa, China, India, South America and even Europe. At the first signs of his wife experiencing labour pains, a husband will retire to his bed and act as if he were giving birth himself – moaning, writhing and demanding attention. Afterwards, he may follow dietary restrictions similar to those of his wife and have a ritual bath.

Although this may appear strange to us, we can all identify with the reasoning behind his actions. The father of an unborn baby will frequently feel excluded from the birth process and may seek to establish a more immediate relationship with his child by involving himself further. Some fathers will even interpret this desire by refraining from any activity they feel may be harmful to their child – for example, using a knife or other sharp implement.

The Celts in Ireland, however, apparently underwent couvade for a different reason. The aim here was for the man to transfer the birth-pangs to himself in order to ease his wife's suffering.

Support
Empathy
Love

Doulas

For countless years, the birthing room has been a place for women only. In addition to the midwife or a local woman experienced in helping at births, many delivering women would also have companions around them to provide emotional support. Women who had previously given birth themselves were felt to have a calming influence on the new mother. These women were known in Greek society as doulas.

Whether you have your baby at home or in hospital, it is very unlikely that any trained personnel will be with you every minute of the labouring period; a doula, however, is there all the time. Women who have a doula present actually require less medication or intervention, and often experience a shorter labour. If you are interested in finding a doula, contact organisations that deal directly with childbirth, your healthcare provider, childbirth educators or lactation consultants.

What she will not do is make your partner feel unwanted or unneccessary. A father may not always be the best birth companion as he is inexperienced with birth and he may be anxious about your safety and the baby's. A good doula, however, will actually help a father to relax and participate more actively in the birth. A birth can mean lots of work for everybody involved, and most fathers like to know there is someone to help should the experience become too overwhelming.

To promote or enhance a positive birth experience, a woman will benefit from continuous support throughout the whole of this trying time – this is what the doula is for! An experienced doula is very knowledgeable about birth and can …

…*Suggest* various positions to make labour and birth more comfortable.

…*Relieve pain* using massage and other non-pharmacological means, helping you to avoid unnecessary medical interventions.

…*Support you* during labour. She will offer you cold or hot packs if required, mop your brow, stay with you, offer encouragement and even give physical support during the pushing.

…*Provide* a written record of the birth, take photos afterwards and advise you on breastfeeding.

You can also contact a doula simply for advice during your pregnancy, for explanations of medical procedures and help with the preparation of a birth-plan.

Lying-in

The first six weeks or so after giving birth are known medically as the puerperium (*puer* means child; *pario* means to bring forth) or, more commonly, the lying-in period. Traditionally, this was a time when new mothers and their babies 'retired' from the world. Mothers could use the time to recuperate from the rigours of birth; babies would begin to learn to adapt to life outside the womb. Today, it is more common for mothers to be up-and-about almost immediately after birth, perhaps showing off their babies to one and all. But maybe we should question whether this is best for mother and baby.

In many traditional cultures, it is recommended that the mother should remain in bed for up to two weeks. In India, both mother and baby remain in bed for 11 days and are then given a ritual bath. A special party is arranged at that time to celebrate the arrival of new life. In Indonesia and Malaysia, the new mother is massaged weekly; oils and special herbs encourage her body to return to its natural condition. The woman's stomach is also wrapped with a sarong to support and strengthen her muscles. In Europe, the resting period is usually up to six weeks, although in many Catholic countries, the custom is for the baby to remain in the home until she is christened.

The trousseau of American colonists included child bedlinen, among which were damask pillow cases for the lying-in. Complete rest in bed will enable the new mother to recover more quickly from the effects of pregnancy and labour. Close family, other relatives and friends all help out with the cooking, cleaning and care of the other children. The mother is encouraged to rest completely. Even activities such as reading a book, watching television or talking on the phone are considered to be too stimulating and thought to detract from the natural healing process. Visitors are also kept to a minimum.

After the birth, your baby needs to be kept quiet so she can get used to her new environment. During this period she should receive little stimulation, stay inside and remain close to you. This is very important because your baby's internal condition is not yet stable and her bones need time to realign themselves after labour. Too many visitors or loud noises can also make her more demanding and fussy. The lying-in period is considered to be a special time for you and your baby, a chance to bond and get to know each other.

After a baby is born, mothers often feel a strong surge of vitality, which can give them a false sense of euphoria. At this time, all a new mother's energy is required to heal her body after the exhausting

Resting

process of labour and delivery. Many mothers make the mistake of feeling so good that they rush to get up, go out shopping or visit friends. If you do not get sufficient rest during the first few weeks, however, you can feel extremely tired and depleted in the months that follow. In addition, if you are feeling tired then the baby will often become more demanding and cranky.

In order to achieve the rest and recuperation you need when your baby is born, it is a good idea to have everything organised before you go into labour. Set up a schedule with your friends and family so that they can come and help with the household duties and cooking. If one person cannot stay the whole time, have different people come on certain days and make a list of things for them to do.

Immediately after you have had your baby, rest in bed as much as you can. Lying horizontally will allow the uterus to return to its normal condition and prevent excessive after-birth bleeding. Bed rest will also help you to produce rich, nourishing milk for your baby. Breastfeeding actually aids in the contraction of the uterus, which is stimulated by the sucking action of the baby. Some women experience strong post-birth contractions, especially after their first child. During these contractions you may find that lying on your stomach is soothing and brings relief.

Keep your daily activities to a minimum and walk around as little as possible. Lying down sends your energy deep inside your body, whereas walking or moving brings your energy to the surface. For at least six weeks think of rest as your priority, along with caring for your

Bonding Healing Nourishing

new baby. Avoid lifting heavy objects and going up and down stairs too much. When you start to go outside, take short walks rather than long ones. Although many new mothers feel impatient during this time and want to do more, lying-in is a time for you to nourish and pamper yourself and your baby. Then, with your renewed strength and vitality, you can relish the joys of motherhood.

Drink to Your Health

Drinking a warm tea known as Kukicha is also beneficial in easing the pain of post-birth contractions. Found in most health food shops, it comes from the twigs of the tea plant and is very mild in flavour. A small amount of rice syrup may be added for a mild, sweet taste. Kukicha can also be fed to your baby with an eye-dropper if she experiences colic. It is a good idea to keep a thermos of tea by your bed in case you get thirsty during the night.

Make sure that you eat a variety of nourishing, healthy foods after delivery and in the following weeks. The extra care you give yourself will ensure the wellbeing of both you and your baby. A balanced diet will speed up your recovery time and help to give you more strength, stamina and vitality. Avoid eating excessive amounts of meat and dairy products. Saturated animal fat causes the uterine tissues to become hard and more rigid, which can create unnecessary pain. Excessive use of cold foods, fruits and sugar will slow down the healing process and can cause prolonged bleeding.

Cultur

Naming Your Baby

The Power and Magic in a Name

There is something very exciting about picking a name for your baby. The sound of a name carries a powerful vibration and will give your baby an identity and a sense of who he is. Choose wisely; bear in mind that your child will carry his given name during his baby years, in school and throughout his adulthood. He will be known to future generations by the name you choose to give him.

Throughout the world, the naming of a baby has great significance, and an amazing amount of care goes into choosing one that fits the character and destiny of the baby. Names are picked for their sound or meaning, in honour of a family member (Greek babies, for example, are always named after a grandparent), to reflect a religion or heritage, or for their astrological or numerological influences.

*If you love someone,
put their name in a circle;
because hearts can be broken,
but circles never end.*

Spirituality Religion Heritage

In Africa, the birth of a child is a time of great joy and the naming of the baby carries much importance. The baby's name represents his character and is a way for him to connect to his cultural past, ancestors and spirituality. When naming the baby, the hopes of the parents, important current events and celestial influences present at the time of birth are all taken into consideration. Africans believe that the name of a baby has a strong influence over his life and that of his family.

Many Eastern cultures used astrologers to help them choose their children's names. In China, for example, a baby's formal name was usually bestowed by his grandparents but, on some occasions, an astrologer would have been consulted. The astrologer would have selected a name to make up for any 'deficiencies' the child's spirit might have, including a lack or excess of the energetic elements of fire, water, metal, wood and earth. These considerations were vital for the survival of the child, because the Chinese believed that a name could influence everything that happened in life. Chinese children are also given a 'milk' name or nickname, which is used until the child starts school and sometimes longer. Boys were often given a girl's name because people believed that evil spirits preyed on boys; if they were given a girl's name, the spirits would be tricked.

In India, many parents record the second, minute and hour of their baby's birth. They then present this information to a Jyotish – a wise person – who uses it to devise the sound of the first syllable of the baby's name. Indians believe that the constant repetition of this sound will affirm the baby's identity in life.

Using
Numerology

When choosing a name for your baby, you can try using the ancient science of numerology. Numerology is not a religion or form of fortune telling; it derives from an understanding that all numbers carry a power and vibration. This science dates back to before the time of Christ. Its history is found not only in the Bible but also in the works of Pythagoras, Plato and other great philosophers.

Through this study of numbers, you can understand a great deal about the inner self. Every letter of the alphabet corresponds to a number between one and nine. You can discover the destiny, character and experience that a name represents by working out the numerical value of that name. Numerology adds an enchanting dimension to the name that you choose to give to your baby.

The easiest way to figure out the numerology of a name is to find the sum total of all the letters. When applying numerology, you have to consider your baby's whole name – the first, middle and surname. Each letter resonates to a specific number; refer to the chart opposite to find the numbers that correspond with the letters of your baby's first, middle and surnames. Then, add together all the numbers in each name and continue to do so until you arrive at one single digit; for an idea, look at the example on the page opposite.

~ *Anna Rose Johnson* ~

Anna 1+5+5+1=12, reduce to a single digit=3   *Rose* 9+6+1+5=21, reduce to a single digit=3

Johnson 1+6+8+5+1+6+5=32, reduce to a single digit=5

Add the three numbers together 3+3+5=11=2   The destiny number for the name Anna Rose Johnson is 2.

Key words for each number

1 = *A J S*   **1** pioneering, individual, enduring, authoritarian, determined, inventive, courageous, self-centred, stubborn, aggressive

2 = *B K T*   **2** diplomatic, peacemaking, kind, loving, refined, considerate, aesthetic, friendly, timid, self-conscious, harmonising

3 = *C L U*   **3** inspirational, imaginative, emotional, joyful, creative, self-expressive, optimistic, selfish, prone to exaggeration, wandering

4 = *D M V*   **4** solid, idealistic, practical, down to earth, reliable, loyal, stubborn, domineering, stuck in a rut

5 = *E N W*   **5** energetic, versatile, resourceful, active, freedom-loving, curious, inventive, changeable, restless, hot-tempered

6 = *F O X*   **6** artistic, loving, humanitarian, altruistic, home-loving, nurturing, harmonising, self-sacrificing, unrelenting, unforgiving, stubborn

7 = *G P Y*   **7** understanding, analytical, contemplative, specialising, charming, intelligent, dignified, inarticulate, repressed, secretive

8 = *H Q Z*   **8** powerful, authoritative, strong, teaching, capable, deep thinking, responsible, materialistic, domineering, ruthless

9 = *I R*   **9** wise, compassionate, forgiving, dramatic, creative, loving, vital, moody, emotional, demanding

75

WELCOMING YOUR BABY ...
NAMING YOUR BABY

Finding the Right Name

When deciding which name to give your baby, take time to discover one that feels right to you; think of ones that have a positive value to you. Search out names that have lovely meanings such as, joy, beauty, strength, wisdom, serenity, vitality or intelligence. Many cultures name their babies after a family member. The eldest child is often named after the father out of respect for the family's heritage. If you feel a family name is not suited to your child, you can always use it as a middle name or pick a variation on the spelling or pronunciation.

Practise saying the first, middle and last name out loud to see if they flow well together. The sound of the name should have a natural feeling to it and not seem awkward or difficult to pronounce. In general, vowels have a more uplifting sound whereas consonants are stronger. A name ending in an 'a', 'y' or 'e' such as Amanda has a bright feeling, and a name that ends with an 'm' or 'n' such as Ian carries a powerful sound. One-syllabled names, such as Paul, have a strong vibration while those with two or more syllables, like Victoria, tend to be softer sounding.

What's in a name? That which we call a rose
By any other name would smell as sweet.

Traditional Naming Ceremonies

Naming traditions vary throughout the world, and sometimes vary depending on whether the baby is a boy or a girl. In Mexico, Seri babies are not named until their first birthday, and on the island of Borneo the Dusin tribe wait five years before naming their children. In Judaism, the naming of a baby boy coincides with the ritual circumcision known as the Bris. It is often the most emotional part of the ceremony. The Bris takes place on the eighth day of the baby's life. The kabbalistic writings teach that seven days represent the physical world of creation. When the child has lived eight days, he transcends from the physical to the metaphysical. Another Jewish tradition is to name the baby after a deceased family member or close friend. This beautiful custom immortalises the person after whom the baby is named.

A Ceremony of Your Own

You can create your own special baby naming ceremony; it doesn't have to be elaborate. Throw a simple party for family and friends to celebrate – share food, honour the birth of your baby and his name. You might like to select suitable prayers and poems or write your own special words that relate to your baby and his new name. Give everyone a small white candle and ask each person to light it to signify new life. Offer small gifts wrapped in red paper or in red envelopes for good luck. In British tradition, silver trinkets – spoons, rattles and keepsakes – are often presented at such a ceremony and help to remind your baby of his special place throughout his life. Make your celebration one to cherish and remember as a unique time for the whole family.

Spiritual Ceremonies

Everywhere in the world, newborn babies have been welcomed using rituals. Birthing ceremonies vary from country to country and depend on the religion practised there. In earlier times, rituals were considered an important part of life, often aligning with the changing seasons and representing strong family and community ties. Although many rituals have been lost, the birth of a baby is still a special and cherished time.

In parts of Africa, children belong not only to their parents but also to the community. The welcoming ceremony introduces the baby to the earth, her ancestors, the heavens and the community. Participants ask for blessings for the baby and give her a taste of a liquor made from corn, so that she can acknowledge the staple food of her ancestors and become part of society. Songs are sung in praise of the baby and to tell her what is expected of her. Friends bring gifts to give her a good start in life and the ceremony ends in a big feast with singing and dancing.

In China, the baby is welcomed with special presents to encourage a long and healthy life. Jade represents health and is often sewn into a hat for the baby to wear. Furthermore, words that represent longevity, health and abundance would be embroidered onto the baby's hat to emphasise these aspects. The Chinese believe the colour red to symbolise happiness and good fortune. Friends and family offer gifts of money in red envelopes and pin these to the baby's clothing. Gold is an obvious representation of wealth and prosperity, and gold jewellery is often given and pinned to the little one's clothes. In both Japan and China, noodles are served at the celebratory dinner because they symbolise long life. Furthermore in Japan, mochi – a dish made from pounded, sticky, sweet rice – may be served to represent the holding together of the family.

One of the most wonderful rituals for greeting a new baby is practised by Native Americans. They hold a beautiful ceremony to welcome her into this world. They introduce her to the earth by placing her feet on the ground. They show the baby the four earthly directions – north, south, east, and west – and hold her up to feel the sun and the wind. Then they place the babe's hand in water and put ash on her forehead to introduce her to the world of elements. Lastly, they hold her up to face the full moon and the stars. Blessings are given to the baby to promote a feeling of belonging and a sense of wonder and connection to her new world.

Your Own Special Celebration

In the West, most babies are baptised or christened, and friends and family gather to welcome them. But you don't have to be religious to welcome your baby's spirit. Create a special welcoming ceremony that is unique to you and your family. If possible, have the ritual outside in a garden or the countryside. Place your baby on the earth and introduce her to nature by showing her water, flowers and trees. Lift her up to wonder at the sun, clouds and the sky. Light white or green candles to represent purity and new beginnings. Create your own special blessings to introduce your baby to her new life and her forefathers, and to tell her the things that are important to you. You could follow the Chinese tradition and give your baby a jade animal for good health; friends and family can bring other gifts wrapped in red paper to honour and give her a happy beginning. End the ceremony with a picnic or buffet to acknowledge the splendour of new life.

Baby Massage

The loving touch a mother gives to her baby is an essential part of his growth and development. Until he learns to talk, a baby uses crying or fussing to communicate his hunger or discomfort. Intuitively, we use touch to reassure, comfort and convey love. These are the essential ingredients for physical and emotional growth and for overall wellbeing. Touch is one of the first sensations a baby experiences and through it, he learns that he is loved. The gentle art of massage can strengthen the bond between you and your baby; nurturing his feelings of security can satisfy your desire to be close to and protect this delicate infant.

Studies have shown that babies who are held, massaged and rocked grow up to have a stronger self-image and are less aggressive than those who aren't. The message of love instilled by massage creates stronger one-to-one communication between you and your baby. As a result, you will develop an intuitive understanding of what your baby needs, and learn where he likes to be stroked.

As well as creating a lovely, calm baby, a simple massage offers many physical benefits. By increasing the flow of oxygen and nutrients to all body cells, massage contributes to a stronger respiratory system and helps your baby to grow and gain weight.

*God could not be everywhere
– so he made mothers.*

It's also great for muscle tone and circulation. Your baby's immune system will become stronger and he'll be able to get rid of toxins more readily. This hands-on approach can soothe your baby's sensitive and immature digestive system, which can cause colic, wind or, later on, teething problems. Gentle rubbing or massaging can provide instant relief from colic or wind by helping your baby feel less tense and by strengthening his digestive system. Research also shows that babies born prematurely gain strength and develop at a much faster rate when they receive a massage on a regular basis. A relaxed, stress-free baby enjoys sounder sleep and for longer periods.

Hands-on Therapy

Massaging a baby is very easy. Initially, you may want simply to slither some warm oil over your baby's skin using very little pressure at all. Once you're more confident, you can learn new strokes and vary the kinds you use. Bear in mind that babies are extremely sensitive and do not need much stimulation. Your touch should convey slight pressure but not be too firm. It's easy to include a massage session in your baby's daily routine; the ideal time is after your baby's bathtime. You can start a few days after he is born and continue well into his first year.

LOOKING AFTER YOUR BABY ...

BABY MASSAGE

Setting the Scene

First and foremost, set a relaxing scene. Make sure the room is warm and free from draughts. Play some quiet music and light a few candles to evoke a sympathetic atmosphere. Warm your oil (see page 85 for which oils to use) by standing the bottle in a bowl of hot water for a few minutes while you get everything else ready. Choose a time when your baby is happy and not tired or hungry. Remove any jewellery, wash your hands and make sure they are warm. Take a few minutes to relax yourself too; your baby will sense any tension in your hands. Sit quietly, breathe deeply and slowly, and shake out your hands.

Making Contact

Now, sit on the floor with your back against a wall for support. Position your baby in your lap, on a towel, so that his feet are pointing toward you and his face is looking up at you – to give him more confidence. Squeeze a few drops of oil onto your palms and slowly rub it all over your baby's body, starting with his shoulders; avoid oiling his hands as they're bound to end up in his mouth. When you feel confident with rubbing oil over your baby, begin to lightly squeeze his limbs starting from the tops of his arms and legs and working down to his hands and feet. Use strokes that work from the centre of the body outward and keep them flowing and smooth. Repeat each stroke at least three times and always keep a light contact with one hand. For a soothing belly rub, use slow, circular strokes in a clockwise direction. During tummytime, massage his back using long strokes that move down the centre of his back to his buttocks and then around and up his sides.

Strengthening Loving Soothing

Stroking your baby's feet can be very important for the relief of colic and wind. If you are too busy to give a full massage, work on the feet alone.

Squeeze and softly press your baby's feet and each of his toes. Rub from the top of his foot and work downwards. Then gently fan out his toes. Working hand-over-hand, pull his whole foot gently and smoothly through your palms, adding more oil to your hands as necessary.

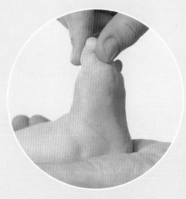

Knead and gently rub the top of your baby's foot with your thumbs.

Roll each of his tiny toes between your forefinger and thumb and tenderly separate.

Flex your baby's ankle and extend the heel of his foot while you gently rub his calf.

Face & Front

When massaging your baby's face, it is not necessary to use oil. Work at drawing your thumbs from the centre of his forehead to the side. Repeat this movement with your thumbs on each side of his nose and draw them to the side and across his cheeks. Finish off with a massage around his mouth. Press lightly from above his upper lip, around the mouth so that your thumbs meet at his chin. Place your hands over his ears and hold them there for about two minutes, allowing your body's heat and energy to transfer to your baby. Complete the massage by lightly brushing over his whole body. Turn your baby over and start on his front. Work from his shoulders down to his hands and then down his back to his feet. Repeat with his front, working from his shoulders down to his hands and from his chest down to his feet. This gentle brushing off will calm your baby and leave him feeling happy and at peace. Remember that a happy baby has a positive effect on his mother, too: you will also feel less stressed, more nourished and more relaxed.

Massage Oils Any vegetable-based oil can form your base oil for massage, but almond oil is ideal because it is easily absorbed. Once your baby is over three months old, and only if he responds well, you could add a few drops of lavender oil to give it a refreshing fragrance. People who live in tropical countries massage with a vegetable oil, which helps to protect the skin during the hot weather, while the gentle stroking and stretching helps the baby to grow stronger. In Portugal and Southern Europe, a popular massage treatment is carried out with olive oil and Portuguese cabbage. This massage is specifically used for digestive troubles and congestion. The olive oil is warmed slightly and then massaged over the baby's stomach. A lightly crushed cabbage leaf is placed on the stomach and secured with a cotton bandage and pins. The cabbage is left for at least two hours and the process is repeated over a few days.

These are baby's fingers,
these are baby's toes;
This is baby's belly button,
round and round it goes.

Magical Baths

Everyone is enthralled with a newborn baby. Watching her take her first bath is a delightful experience and one that can be enjoyed by others – grandparents, siblings and friends. A bath is also a great way to help your baby calm down and unwind, as well as smoothly discharging excess minerals and toxins. For practical reasons, it is a good idea to bath your baby on a daily basis and at the same time each day. An established routine will make her feel stable and secure. Giving her a bath can help her relax at the times when she is most fussy.

Most babies love their bath and, because mother and child are so close, bathtime will help you to feel calm and refreshed, too. You can make each bath a magical occasion, one in which you and your baby spend precious moments together in a quiet and peaceful environment. To make this routine even more enchanting, you can bathe together.

Tiny babies can often feel afraid if they experience sudden changes in temperature or lighting. Undressing them, placing them in water and then taking them out of the bath could be quite a shock and she may cry or become agitated. By being in the bath, you make your baby feel safe – she can see you all the time – and she can learn to enjoy her bathtime sessions from day one.

The tiny perfect fingernails ...
were like the small pink shells scuffed up
in the sands of tropical beaches.

Enchanting Surroundings

For hassle-free bathtimes with your baby, get everything you'll need ready beforehand. Place a thick bath towel on the floor near the bath. A hooded baby towel is perfect for wrapping your little one after her bath, so lay this on top of the bath towel. Grab some clean pyjamas as well as a nappy, and keep them handy. If you're taking a dip, too, then don't forget a big thick towel for yourself and a warm bathrobe.

Create a relaxing atmosphere in the bathroom. Make sure that the room is warm enough, as babies are extremely sensitive to draughts. Candlelight is exquisite to bathe by. Candles are calming and their gentle flickering light creates a lovely, comforting air. Choose fragrance-free candles; those with added scent may be too strong for your baby. If you wish to play background music, choose pieces that are soothing or use cheerful baby lullabies.

Soap isn't necessary for a newborn's delicate skin but everyone enjoys washing a baby. If you wish to use soap, then choose one with a vegetable oil base and little or no fragrance; or you may prefer to try the simple oatmeal sachets, see page 89.

Slippery When Wet

Fill the bath with water. Make sure that the temperature is comfortably warm by dipping in your elbow or wrist. Place a cotton washcloth on the edge of the bath so you can reach it easily. At first, you may need your partner or a family member to hand your baby to you in the bath, but with time you'll gain confidence and can have her all to yourself.

Lay your baby on her back, leaning on your stomach for support, and gently wash her all over. In the first few weeks take care to keep her navel dry: ensure the water level is below her tummy. As she relaxes, her fingers will unclench and her limbs will splay outwards. Be patient if she cries or seems agitated; some babies take time to get used to bathing.

When it is time to take your little bundle out of the bath, hand her back to your partner. Hold her arms gently at her sides and remove her quickly so that she can be covered with the towel. Wrap her up well and give her a cuddle. A baby's skin is sensitive so pat it dry rather than rubbing. Then, inhale the delicious fragrance of her newly washed skin.

A baby lotion is good for dry skin, but, as with soap, it is not necessary. If you want to use lotion, choose one with a vegetable base and little or no fragrance. Olive or almond oil, with added aloe vera, is mild enough to use as an alternative to baby lotion.

Older siblings will also relish a bath with their little brother or sister; initially, bathtimes can help older children connect with the new arrival, and later on older brothers or sister can encourage play and make-believe in their magical baths. As she grows, bathing becomes a time for fun and play, so invest in some brightly coloured toys such as yellow ducks or wooden boats. Babies love experimenting with water: a few plastic cups for pouring water provide endless entertainment.

Oatmeal is known for its wonderful skin-softening properties. Pop an easy-to-make oatmeal sachet in your bath water and both you and your baby will relish the benefits.

For the sachet

20cm square of material (cheesecloth or cotton)
1 tablespoon of oatmeal
Some string or an elastic band

1 Cut a piece of cheesecloth into a square; you could use a pure cotton handkerchief as an alternative.

2 Place a heaped tablespoon of oatmeal in the centre of the square.

3 Gather up the sides and twist them once.

4 Secure the bundle by tying it tightly with a piece of string or with an elastic band.

5 When the bath is ready, drop one or more sachets into the water. Squeeze them a few times to release the creamy, oaty liquid. You can also gently dab the sachet on your baby or yourself.

Feeding and Bonding

Parental love develops after birth through taking care of the baby. Both mother and child (and father and child) experience feelings of comfort, happiness and satisfaction when feeding. From this emotional perspective, it's not so much whether you choose to feed from the breast or the bottle that is important, but the atmosphere you create for nursing your baby; this time is vital for creating and reinforcing the physical, psychological and spiritual bond between you.

Breastfeeding is the most natural and beautiful way that you and your baby can develop a strong and loving bond. Breast milk contains the perfect balance of nutrition, which also nourishes your tiny infant on many levels. As well as a combined food and drink, breast milk confers natural immunity to a number of infections through the colostrum – the fluid that comes in before the real milk. Breast milk in general helps the baby to develop a strong immune system, is easy to digest and assimilate, and gives the baby a strong, healthy start in life.

There is a very practical side to breastfeeding too: it is inexpensive and especially convenient. There aren't any bottles to prepare, wash or sterilise. Travelling and visiting friends is easy because no prior food preparation is needed. Breast milk contains natural tranquilising chemicals and so helps your baby to calm down and fall asleep; this is particularly useful for the night feeds of the first few months. What's more you can stay in bed while you breastfeed; your baby can nurse straight away and his sleep pattern is less disturbed. Breast milk also contains endorphins, which suppress pain. If your baby feels discomfort or is hurting in some way, he will feel instantly soothed and relaxed after a few minutes of suckling at your breast.

Many first-time mothers are nervous about breastfeeding. If you are worried about your milk supply, try to relax and get enough rest in the first few weeks. Milk production works on a supply and demand basis: the more your baby nurses, the more milk you produce. As your baby grows and develops, he will empty the breast more completely, which stimulates the increase in supply. You'll gain confidence when you see the round, well-nourished appearance of your baby, knowing that the gift of health has come from you alone.

The many natural advantages to breastfeeding mean that it's worth giving it a good try in the first few weeks, before switching to bottle-feeding. Sometimes, however, breastfeeding isn't an option and it's best all round if the baby is fed via a bottle. Babies can grow well and thrive on formula milk, and feeding times can still be a pleasurable experience during which you and your baby become closer and more contented. Bottlefeeding also offers a chance for a partner to bond with his baby.

Mind & Body

As well as nourishing your baby's body, feeding also satisfies your baby's emotional needs. All babies develop at a faster rate when held and cuddled regularly. It is hard to find a replacement for the comforting feeling that a baby receives when held close; skin to skin contact is an instant soother and helps to strengthen the parental bond. Feeding on demand helps your baby to feel safe and secure; it satisfies his sucking instinct and he can suck as long as he needs to.

Love

Connect

Protect

Nurture

If you choose to breastfeed, you too will benefit greatly. Your baby's sucking action aids the contraction of the womb. Nursing stimulates the release of the hormone oxytocin in the mother's body, which stimulates uterine contraction and boosts milk supply. This, in turn, helps you to regain your energy and strength more quickly. Oxytocin also promotes maternal behaviour and the bonding between you and your little one. Nursing actually increases the body's ability to lose weight and helps a woman return to her pre-pregnancy figure more rapidly. Not only does your baby benefit from the natural tranquilisers in the breast milk, it also helps you to feel relaxed, calm and emotionally secure.

Creating the Perfect Atmosphere

It is important to enjoy the time that you feed your baby. While at home, you can create a relaxed, loving environment for you both to spend quality time together. If you feel tense and nervous, listen to some soothing music and breathe slowly and deeply before you feed; your baby is receptive to your tension and it could spoil feeding times. Make sure you are comfortable: this could be in your favourite armchair or lying on your bed. Use pillows to support your arm and the baby's head; even if you're bottlefeeding, cradling your baby so that his cheek is next to the skin of your breast is a highly pleasurable and worthwhile experience. Relish this personal time with your baby, turn the lights down low, light candles and enjoy peaceful music. Even if he falls asleep during feeding times, it is a good idea to burp him – otherwise he may wake up a few minutes later restless.

Make eye contact with your baby to strengthen the bond between you. But once deep into feeding, he may close his eyes, fully relaxed and at home in your arms. Hold his gaze while cuddling and feeding him; he'll soon develop a trust in you and feel more secure.

Feeding is a deeply moving sensation that strengthens the bond with your baby. Watching him develop is a wonderful experience that will fill your heart with pride and joy. It aligns you with the natural process of life and you feel and understand the miracle of motherhood.

Wondrous Playthings

Toys are the tools with which your baby can begin to gently stimulate his senses – sight, touch, hearing, smell and taste – as well as perfecting his motor development. By playing with you, he develops a natural curiosity and love of learning. During the first month, your baby won't be interested in toys, instead he wants to look at your face, especially your eyes; at this time, he can see only 20–25cm away, so make sure you meet his gaze within this distance. As he grows older, he will begin to move his head and follow a moving image. He can move his arms with a bit of purpose and can hold objects that are easy to grab for a short time. He next discovers his hands and feet – these provide hours of fun.

When he is two to three months old, you can begin to introduce simple toys and to show him interesting things. Young babies may seem quiet, but they are alert and ready to learn. Keep your baby's life quietly stimulating including sounds, smells, sights and things to touch: brightly coloured toys attract his attention, while wooden toys are smooth to the touch. Play with an easy-going attitude; if your baby looks away or fusses, take a break. By four months or so, he will start to reach and grab with some accuracy and hold objects with both hands. Also, he'll begin to understand that he feels differently with different people, such as being excited with his brother or sister or feeling calm when held by you.

You do not need to give your baby lots of toys. Too many toys can be overstimulating and cause confusion and frustration. Give him only comfortable amounts of activity. Learn to read his reactions: stop or change activities if he seems upset or frustrated. Too much stimulation at this age is not helpful for the growth and development of his brain.

One of the first toys that you can give your baby is a rattle. These are perfect for tiny hands to grasp, hold and inspect, plus their noise when shaken delights your baby. Rattles come in many shapes and sizes, and help your baby learn that his hands are useful. Dolls, another first toy favourite, can also be simple in shape and form, in fact those without distinct features help to develop your baby's imagination. There are many dolls that are made from a soft fabric such as velour and are perfect for babies and small children. Select soft dolls that rattle and have bendy arms and legs – ideal to explore with his hands or mouth.

Toys don't have to be expensive. Small babies love to play with everyday items that are part of the home like wooden spoons, and things from nature, such as pine cones or large shells. Dolls can easily be made out of socks and animals from bean bags. Where possible, play and have fun with your baby on the floor or outside on the grass. Plenty of exercise on the floor will develop your baby's sense of balance.

Remedies for Babies

You know your baby best and will be tuned into his different cries and behaviour. The strong bond between you means you will soon know intuitively when he is feeling unwell. Illness in babies can provoke a great deal of anxiety, especially when they are tiny and their immune systems not fully developed. This anxiety is a protective mechanism so that you watch ever-more cautiously over your precious little bundle.

As your baby meets your friends and family, he will be exposed to germs. Of course, it's a good idea to keep him away from those with obvious infections, but colds are almost unavoidable. If he's having difficulty breathing, use a vaporiser with some eucalyptus oil in his room; alternatively you could place a few drops onto his clothes or the mattress of his cot. For a homeopathic remedy use *Aconite* two to three times a day from the first day of the cold. For sneezy colds with a runny nose use *Nat mur,* and for colds with a fever try *Merc. sol.*

The thick scaly dandruff of cradle cap is a common sight in a baby's early months. If your baby has a touch of this, then dab some olive oil onto the affected area and leave for a couple of hours to soften the scales. Rub firmly with a dry towel and then wash off and dry his hair.

Who ran to help me when I fell,
And would some pretty story tell.
Or kiss the place to make it well,
My Mother.

Babies have very small tubes in their ears and it is easy for these to get clogged and cause pain. If you are breastfeeding your baby, you could squeeze a few drops of breast milk into the ear to help alleviate the pain and clear the tubes. Other remedies include some cotton wool with one drop of lavender oil plugged into the ear or the juice of pennywort leaves dropped into the ear and sealed with cotton wool. Give ABC – a mixture of *Aconite*, *Belladonna* and *Camomile* – when you suspect earache.

Often, a new baby develops sticky eyes. Squeeze a few drops of breast milk into your baby's eyes and the condition will clear up quickly. Or you could gently bathe his eyes in a weak salt solution (1 teaspoon of salt to 300ml of water) using a fresh piece of cotton wool each time.

Few babies escape their first few months without a rash. Most rashes appear as a reaction to the time spent in the womb and will eventually disappear. You can treat thrush – the rash caused by yeast inside the mouth and/or on the bottom – with the liquid from garlic pearls.

Dreamcatchers

The Native Americans have a beautiful legend that they believed helped create a deep and peaceful sleep. The Ancient Ones would tell that dreams have great power and float about at night before coming to the sleeping ones. To protect the dreamer, the Ancient Ones created a special web – the dreamcatcher – to hang above their sleeping places. Dreamcatchers were placed over a baby's cradle with the idea that the good spirit dreams, being clever, would find their way through the central hole in the web and float down the sacred feathers onto the sleeping baby. The bad spirit dreams, being stupid, would get hopelessly entangled in the web and perish with the morning light. Dreamcatchers were also believed to bestow on the baby good luck and harmony, and were a way to strengthen the link between creation and the spirit world.

Dreamcatchers were made to look like spiders' webs as they catch and hold evil just as real webs ensnare unwitting insects. In some legends, babies have catchers made of willow and sinew, which would then dissolve like the innocence of youth. Original dreamcatchers were made from wooden hoops and woven nettle-stalk cord, dyed red from bloodroot and the bark of wild plum. Later, they became more intricate, being made from yarn, beads, feathers and leather. Small beads were believed to be the good dreams caught by Mother Sun at star time.

Beads
Ribbons
Feathers

Mother's Music

Throughout the ages, mothers have rocked their babies to sleep with gentle humming, songs and simple melodies, known as lullabies. The word lullaby has deep roots in the English language: *lulla* means to soothe and *bye* is an old word for sleep. Lullabies are very effective in helping a baby to calm down or fall asleep because of their simply orchestrated format. Newborn babies seem to relax more quickly when they are listening to female voices and they prefer their own mother's voice above everything. The unique characteristics of lullabies – regular, monotonous and repetitive – are especially suited to babies. They are sung in a low voice with no disruptions in the rhythm or melody.

When a baby is held near to his mother's heart, he feels more secure, relaxed and calm. The beat of a lullaby is slow and steady, much the same as a resting adult heartbeat. Lullabies therefore create the same message of safety and comfort for the baby. Soft drumming can also be used because the sound and rhythm is again similar to a heartbeat.

Sleep, baby, sleep!
Thy father's watching the sheep,
Thy mother's shaking the dreamland tree,
And down drops a little dream for thee,
Sleep, baby, sleep.

Musical Interludes

Music can also be played while your baby is actually sleeping. A baby will feel comforted by pieces that you listened to during your pregnancy. A large selection of music is not necessary. In fact, a baby feels happier when listening to one or two familiar recordings. Listening to music is a lovely way in which you and your baby can feel connected, uplifted and at peace. Classical music, such as Mozart, has also helped to reduce depression and stress. Musical boxes are also enchanting and can be placed in the baby's nursery. They come in an array of shapes and sizes. Choose ones that have a clear, beautiful tone and that play lullabies.

The Mbuti of Zaire sing lullabies to their babies; these are the only songs they can sing solo, and they are composed for a newborn by her mother. They are sung for no other and sung by no other.

Recent research has shown that premature babies react positively when music is played to them. It helps them to increase their oxygen intake, sleep better and develop at a faster rate. The choice of music for all babies and especially fragile, premature babies should be carefully considered. Music with simple, gentle rhythms and flowing, lyrical melodies is ideal, along with simple harmonies and a soft tone. Babies react positively to simple tunes with a low pitch. High pitches tend to create tension and are disturbing to small babies and young children.

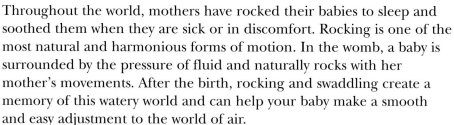

The Art of Rocking

Throughout the world, mothers have rocked their babies to sleep and soothed them when they are sick or in discomfort. Rocking is one of the most natural and harmonious forms of motion. In the womb, a baby is surrounded by the pressure of fluid and naturally rocks with her mother's movements. After the birth, rocking and swaddling create a memory of this watery world and can help your baby make a smooth and easy adjustment to the world of air.

Rocking helps to regulate the heart beat and strengthens natural balance. It creates a feeling of safety and security and is a relaxing activity for both mother and baby. Holding, rocking and cuddling give a child a stronger sense of self and help her to develop confidence and personal boundaries. If a baby is rocked from birth, her sense of balance will be strengthened and she will be able to master walking more quickly. This is important for all physical activities, as a child with a strong sense of balance can move from one kind of terrain to another with ease, such as from grass to a concrete path or over rocks. Rocking also helps a child to develop courage and agility.

During your pregnancy, you can enjoy the gentle pleasure of rocking in a garden or on a porch. Garden centres offer a variety of rocking seats and hammocks that can be hung or set up to give you

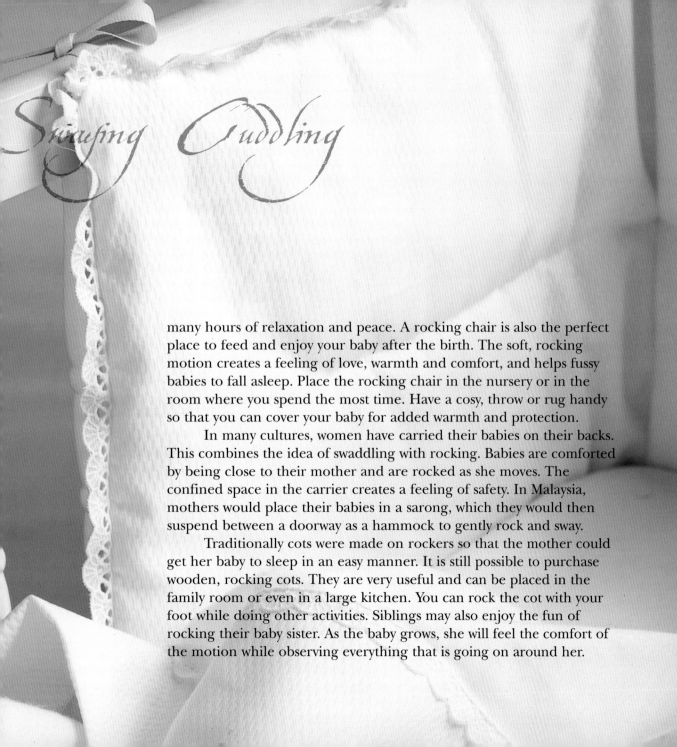

Swaying Cuddling

many hours of relaxation and peace. A rocking chair is also the perfect place to feed and enjoy your baby after the birth. The soft, rocking motion creates a feeling of love, warmth and comfort, and helps fussy babies to fall asleep. Place the rocking chair in the nursery or in the room where you spend the most time. Have a cosy, throw or rug handy so that you can cover your baby for added warmth and protection.

In many cultures, women have carried their babies on their backs. This combines the idea of swaddling with rocking. Babies are comforted by being close to their mother and are rocked as she moves. The confined space in the carrier creates a feeling of safety. In Malaysia, mothers would place their babies in a sarong, which they would then suspend between a doorway as a hammock to gently rock and sway.

Traditionally cots were made on rockers so that the mother could get her baby to sleep in an easy manner. It is still possible to purchase wooden, rocking cots. They are very useful and can be placed in the family room or even in a large kitchen. You can rock the cot with your foot while doing other activities. Siblings may also enjoy the fun of rocking their baby sister. As the baby grows, she will feel the comfort of the motion while observing everything that is going on around her.

Swaddling

As an age-old remedy for fussing or colicky babies, mothers all over the world wrap their babies tightly in shawls or blankets to give them a sense of security and tranquillity. New babies particularly benefit from having their limbs restrained for a short period of time. Firm, steady pressure can quieten your baby and interfere with his startle reflex action. The startle reflex is a remnant of our early ancestry. A baby who experiences a sudden change in position will think he is falling. He will start to cry, drop his head backwards, extend his neck and throw his arms and legs outwards before rapidly bringing them back together as if to clasp his mother and save himself. In doing so, he becomes disturbed, and sets off the startle reflex again in a vicious circle. Steady pressure on his body will calm him down.

Baby, sleep a little longer
Till thy little limbs are stronger...

Most babies enjoy having their arms and legs secured but you can also keep your baby's arms free so that he can suck his fingers, if he likes. A receiving blanket, shawl or any large piece of gauzy material will work just fine.

1 Fold your receiving blanket or shawl into a triangle. Lay your baby down in the centre so that his neck aligns with the fold at the top.

2 Pull one side of the blanket over his shoulder and diagonally across his body. Bring the corner under his other arm and tuck it under his bottom.

3 Take the opposite corner and pull it over your baby's other shoulder. If you like, tuck his arm up against his neck so that he can reach his mouth with his thumb.

4 Fold the material neatly under his body so that he is held securely. Check that the blanket is not too tight around his neck.

5 Finally, gather together the open folds at the bottom and tuck the material underneath to cover his feet. If your baby is not already fast asleep, he soon will be.

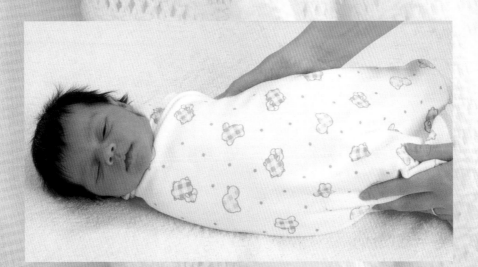

Herbal Soothers

Scented toys are ideal sleep-inducers for fractious babies and infants. They can be tucked near to the cot, strung across a pram hood or, for older children, placed underneath a pillow. There are many slumber-promoting herbs: hops, lemon balm, lime flowers, catmint and lavender are among the best known.

Calming Camomile

Older babies and children may also benefit from a night-time tea, particularly if they are excitable and unable to relax before sleep. An important ingredient here is camomile. In medieval times, bunches of camomile flowers were hung over babies' cradles to protect them from infection and keep them happy and healthy. Camomile has a lovely relaxing effect, calming tension and anxiety, and aiding sleep. When babies or children are unwell and feverish, it can soothe them to sleep, which is nature's best medicine, enabling their bodies to carry out their healing work unhampered and thereby speeding recovery. Camomile is also wonderful for easing childhood fears, especially at night, and helps to prevent nightmares.

For the scented toy

Cardboard or stiff paper
1 metre of cotton fabric or fabric leftovers
1 metre of lining material
Dried herbs: your choice of lavender, hops,
    lemon balm, lime flowers and catmint
Crushed cardamom seeds
Crushed cloves
Orris root powder, optional
Lavender or lemon balm oil, optional
Ribbon leftovers

1 Draw simple outlines of animals, such as bears, ducks, fish or cats, on cardboard to use as templates.

2 For each animal, cut out a front and back from the cotton fabric and another front and back, 5mm smaller all round, from the lining material.

3 Sew the lining fabric to the wrong side of the outer fabric. Then, with the right sides facing, sew the animal's front to its back, leaving about 2.5cm unstitched.

4 Turn the animal right-side-out and stuff with the herb selection. Add some crushed cardamom seeds and cloves and, if desired, a pinch of orris root powder and a drop of lavender or lemon balm oil.

5 Stitch the open seam closed. You can add further decoration in the form of embroidered or appliqued features and neat ribbon bows.

Herbal soother

Lavender

Lime Flowers

Catmint

Cardamom

Cloves

Astrological Signs

The importance of astrology in many traditional cultures is based on the understanding that a baby's destiny is strongly influenced by his date of conception and birth. The principles guiding their studies are founded on the innumerable changes that the earth goes through on a daily, monthly and yearly basis, as well as the vibrational influences received from the celestial sphere. These influences will affect the quality of the sperm and the egg, as well as the type of activity and diet that the mother is attracted to during her pregnancy.

A baby born in springtime will have a physical and mental constitution opposite to that of a child who is born during the autumn. A spring baby will be strongly affected by the autumn and winter months, because he was in the womb during that time. A baby born in the autumn, on the other hand, will be influenced more strongly by the spring and summer months. Your baby's star sign can help you to discover your child's potential. It can help you to assess your baby's soon-to-be strengths and weaknesses, and to anticipate some areas of conflict and harmony within your family. Bear in mind, however, that this is only a reflection of his potential.

Aries – 21 March to 20 April

The child born under the sign of the ram will be optimistic, independent, assertive, energetic and 'me' orientated. He can be hot tempered, strong willed, impetuous and very competitive. This child will always be on the go. He will demonstrate little fear and a lot of courage. Bossy but affectionate, your child will also forgive slights easily. The Aries child does not respond well to restrictive discipline, so when he's troublesome the best approach will be to distract him with something new to do or to play with.

Taurus – 21 April to 21 May

Your Taurean child is certain to be a contented one, smiling when you take him out of his crib and being delighted with his food. Loyal and loving, your baby will enjoy cuddles and can be quite charming. One of the fixed signs of the zodiac, Taureans are conservative and welcome discipline; they respond best to having a schedule set for things. Your baby likes security and will hate having his routine disrupted. Sometimes slow to learn, when he does master walking or crawling, it will be performed with competency. Your child will be stubborn and a bit of a plodder, but he will never give up. He will probably have a powerful temper, which is lit by a slow fuse.

Gemini – 22 May to 21 June

Born under the sign of the twins, your baby will be a live wire, mischievous, curious and inventive. He will rarely sit still and will appear to run on nervous energy. Your child may have a short attention span but will be creative, playful, communicative and have a good sense of humour. Quite independent, he won't sit still for cuddles. Certain to talk – and walk – early, it is important to supply your baby with lots of different stimulating things to do, but don't be surprised if his interest doesn't last long; he gets fed up fairly easily. Unfortunately, when a Gemini gets bored, he can make your life miserable!

Cancer – 22 June to 23 July

Don't be surprised if your baby exhibits a lot of sensitivity to your mood, even when quite young. Cancerians are very intuitive and respond quickly to change. Home-loving and possessive of family members, your baby will demand cuddles. He will be quite possessive of things and your attention. Cancerians are known for hoarding and being untidy. Your baby will have a crab-like approach to life, that is being oblique in action and hiding his ambitions and feelings, so it is vital to remember he is highly sensitive, insecure and often moody. When disciplining, you should always try to call upon his sensitivity to things and people.

Leo – 24 July to 23 August

Fiery but fixed in nature, the Leo baby can be a delight with a sunny disposition and lots of enthusiasm. He will crave attention but is highly affectionate and is quite happy to show it. While loving and playful, he can also be dominating, demanding, stubborn and full of pride. This pride, however, can be deflated easily, so you must use affection and humour when disciplining him. Though your baby likes routine, he is also highly creative; dressing-up and performing – particularly before an audience – is one of things he will like best.

Virgo — 24 August to 23 September

This baby will make you the envy of other parents. He will be well behaved, clean, tidy and obedient. Observant, intellectual and practical by nature, Virgoans like being given things to do. Although your baby may appear unemotional, he is really very shy and sensitive, and enjoys solitude. He will have a propensity to be picky about food, fussy over his health and generally critical of most things, particularly his own efforts, so it's important to be calm and relaxed and not to draw too much attention to things. You need to help build up your child's self-confidence as he can easily become upset over little things.

Libra — 24 September to 23 October

Affectionate, sensual, charming and flirtatious, your baby enjoys relationships and cuddles, and tries hard to please. He enjoys family harmony and likes companionship. Very tactful, a Libran tries to avoid upsets and will even lie to save hurting others. Laid back by nature, he will procrastinate over decisions and often seems indecisive and lazy. This is because they are looking at all sides of a question, seeking justice and fairness. Your child may find it hard to say 'no' and you will need to build his confidence and ability to make his own decisions.

Scorpio — 24 October to 22 November

Deep, strong willed and secretive, your child will be an intensely private person, loyal to a fault, with a tendency to keep his feelings bottled up. This should not be encouraged, particularly as Scorpios have a strong sense of justice and often think they are being punished unfairly. Your baby may be jealous and possessive, and have a bit of a temper. He will thrive on security and routine. He will have a powerful imagination and enjoy getting involved in many activities. He is perceptive and insightful about others, but does not necessarily enjoy sharing such feelings.

Sagittarius — 23 November to 21 December

Generous and enthusiastic, your child is a natural explorer, loving independence, freedom and space. He will be curious and will exhibit no fear, but will also be careless, boisterous and lack discipline. In fact, he will become unhappy if tied down to a routine. Frank, spontaneous, talkative and friendly, a Sagittarian child asks a lot of questions and will enjoy learning. The more you praise him, the more he will respond. Don't expect too much overt affection from him but he will enjoy playing games with you, especially if they are of a sporty nature.

Capricorn — 22 December to 20 January

Serious, cautious, responsible and self-contained, your child will work hard and obey the rules. He will need a secure, structured environment. Capricorn infants are loyal and take pride in their parents, who need to live up to expectations! While your child may seem pessimistic, this is

If you can command yourself, you can command the world.

offset by a keen sense of humour and an enjoyment of life, which needs to be nurtured. Your child will also enjoy learning about the past and being involved in seasonal traditions. Ambitious and money-orientated, your child will not be afraid to put himself forward.

Aquarius – 21 January to 19 February
Unpredictable, rebellious, independent and broad-minded, your baby will be a real trend-setter. Oblivious to time, he will be fascinated by the unusual and will seek to experiment in all things. Generally happy and positive, your baby will be empathetic but emotionally detached, withdrawing from cuddles. Aquarian children can be somewhat surly and sometimes it's best to suggest that they do the opposite of what you really want. They can be very trusting of strangers, so you must caution your child about this when he is old enough to understand.

Pisces – 20 February to 20 March
Dreamy, artistic, sympathetic and enamoured of fantasy, your baby will be emotionally expressive, delighting in comfort and cuddles. Easily influenced but disliking responsibility, it is important to set boundaries so that he does not confuse play-acting for reality. Piscean children often need to be on their own as they have a private inner world, which to them is a very special and precious place. They are happiest when devoted to another person, however, as they are very compassionate people. Parents need to take a strong line, encouraging their children to be truthful, honest and straightforward.

Chinese Animals

The ancient art of Chinese astrology has been used for thousands of years as a way to understand the inner nature of people. There are 12 different signs, each represented by an animal. In Chinese legend, Buddha chose these symbolic animals to represent 12 different types or combinations of energy. Each year corresponds to one particular animal, and the date for the new year begins around the end of January to the middle of February, which aligns with the lunar calendar.

Chinese astrology holds many clues to help you understand your baby's emotional, mental and spiritual nature. Whether she is a tiger or a dragon, these signs can help you to nurture her potential. The Chinese animals recur over a continuous 12-year cycle. To work out the animal with which your little one resonates, check the year dates next to the animal descriptions to see which matches her birthday year. If you wish to find another date, add or subtract 12 from the years shown.

The Rat – 2008, 2020

The first symbolic animal chosen by the Buddha was the rat. This sign represents the ability for leadership. Your rat baby will turn into a charming, intelligent and also affectionate child. She makes friends easily, is very helpful and can concentrate for long periods on detailed work. A quick learner, she is ambitious at school and will participate in anything that stimulates her mental ability. Rats are survivors and may sometimes appear crafty and calculating in order to get what they want. Your child values and loves her parents dearly, and her childhood will generally be a happy and joyful one.

The Ox – 2009, 2021

This sign also resonates with the much less domesticated buffalo. A baby born in this year will be the strong silent type with a born sense of responsibility and self-discipline. She can appear very stubborn and obstinate, and thrives on a schedule or set routine. The ox child can be outspoken and strong willed but, at the same time, she is also naive about the realities of life and needs protection and a lot of moral support from both parents and teachers. She takes her school studies seriously (sometimes too seriously) and should be encouraged to express her feelings and develop her sense of humour.

The Tiger – 2010, 2022

Your tiger child has boundless energy and enthusiasm; you could liken her to Tigger from the Winnie the Pooh stories. She sparkles with activity and is always in the thick of things. At a young age, the tiger does not like following orders and can also be a holy terror. Even though she is very warm, loving and affectionate, your infant does need to be disciplined and given boundaries in order to keep her emotional nature in check. Life with a tiger child may not run as smoothly as you wish but this vivacious, lively and spontaneous little minx will entertain and charm you throughout her childhood.

The Rabbit — 2011, 2023

The even-tempered and obedient rabbit child is also sensitive, peaceful and well mannered. Good in school, she enjoys a good debate and will be able to take account of both sides of an argument. Her sensitivity can occasionally cause her some anxiety and trouble sleeping. A rabbit child has a smooth way of speaking and can convert you to her way of thinking without you even realising she has done so. On the whole, she has an abundance of friends who enjoy her calm, dependable manner and her never-ending ability simply to shrug off her problems and start again from the beginning, if necessary.

The Dragon — 2000, 2012

The mythical dragon never ceases to enchant and stir the imagination. This high-spirited child is intelligent, charismatic and vibrant. She is quick to learn, enjoys challenges and has a somewhat idealistic view of life. The dragon child needs to feel useful, otherwise her intense, passionate and domineering nature will get the better of her. She loves to be needed and will go to great lengths to please you and gain your respect. It is important to praise your dragon child as she can be hard on herself. This is a proud, self-sufficient child who stands by her ideals.

A child's life is like a piece of paper on which every person leaves a mark.

The Snake — 2001, 2013

By nature this quiet, mysterious creature has inborn wisdom and a sharp penetrating mind. The snake child takes care of herself and can be quite possessive of the attention given by her parents and friends. She plays well by herself and enjoys imaginative games. She is not prone to self-expression and can hide her true feelings, which can cause her to bear grudges and not forgive easily. She is able to stick to a task until she masters it and is practical about setting goals. Her wise, reserved personality stands her in good stead for long-lasting friendships.

The Horse — 2002, 2014

This beautiful, versatile and flexible animal confers a lively and animated personality on your little one. Her childhood years will be full of adventure and joy. She learns quickly; if she's held back she becomes stubborn and difficult. Horses love exercise and the outdoor life, so a horse child will not fare well with too many rules and regulations, although she needs to learn to check her temper. Her independence will be evident from early on and she knows how to get herself out of trouble. A horse child has a restless, searching nature but she does adapt and conform when she finds there is no easy way out.

Emotional

The Sheep – 2003, 2015

With an air of contentment and sincerity, a sheep child will be a joy to her parents and loves to be cuddled and fussed over. This child needs security, love and encouragement in all her actions. She appreciates art, beauty and nature and is very sensitive. A sheep child is attached to her parents and is likely to cling to them for support. She views the world as a beautiful, magical place and has a naturally compassionate and generous attitude towards her friends. Teasing or criticism may cause her sorrow, and she will need lots of sympathy to lift her spirits again.

The Monkey – 2004, 2016

A baby born in the year of the monkey will have a great sense of fun and mischief. She is always on the move and never misses a trick. She likes to take things apart to see how they work and is full of questions on every subject. The monkey is interested in lots of activities and is never satisfied: the grass always looks greener somewhere else. Your monkey child may have a selfish streak and does not like to share, yet feels perfectly happy taking other children's toys. She is very optimistic and enjoys challenges and opportunities.

The Rooster – 2005, 2017

Your child will be resilient and rather eccentric. Roosters are very neat and orderly and are always looking for answers. A rooster child tends to speak her mind and can be bossy and critical. This is a demanding child but one who is also very helpful and organised. The rooster is full of schemes and ideas and it is hard to change her mind once it is made up. She is never content to take the middle road and her childhood may be a roller-coaster ride. An extremely good student, your little chick will show an interest in money at an early age.

The Dog — 2006, 2018

Regarded as man's best friend, the dog is loyal, honest and noble. A dog baby is well-behaved, affectionate and loving. Playful and humorous, she stays close to home even though she likes a degree of independence. Your child will tackle school work with an easy and sensible attitude. She needs plenty of praise and encouragement, otherwise she may lose confidence and self-esteem. If she is pushed too far, this puppy will retaliate with a temper that erupts and then subsides quickly. It is hard to reason with her; she can be unbending and opinionated. That said, this friendly child will always put family and home first.

The Boar — 2007, 2019

In the Chinese horoscope, being a boar is an honour and a compliment. A boar child is a model of sincerity, tolerance and trust. Early on, the boar's pleasure-seeking ways are evident as she puts her friends and interests first. The boar is very strong and can suffer pain without complaining. She excels in groups and shows a great passion for living. The boar child will be extremely loyal to her friends and family and has a natural understanding for another's emotions or needs, which at times can seem wise beyond her years.

Face Reading

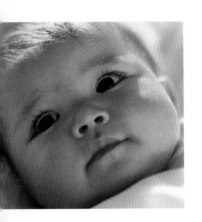

In ancient Japan, China, Korea and India, a system of visual diagnosis developed that was used as a way of life. At its centre was the understanding that everything reflects the whole, and that the body works together as one unique system. Visual diagnosis is a great way to understand your baby's condition at birth and his constitutional nature. Learning to analyse your baby will give you an insight into his true nature and can be used to help him develop his innate talents. Visual analysis is a positive approach to life and aids you in gently guiding the destiny of your child. If he appears to be lacking in some area, it should not be viewed as a negative or bad thing, rather a learning tool to help him to grow and develop on the path to health and happiness.

When a baby is born he should have a strong, clear cry. Boys tend to have a loud, penetrating cry and girls a softer, more gentle cry. Although crying can be an indication of hunger or some kind of discomfort, it also is the way a baby releases frustration and stress. Babies cannot run around or shout in order to discharge excess energy. Allowing your baby to cry for short periods will help him to strengthen his lungs and relax his body. However, it is important not to let your baby cry for long periods of time.

The hands of a newborn will usually be curled up into tightly clenched fists. A healthy baby has a strong, tight grasp when he holds your finger. The baby's fingers are an indication of his artistic and mental development: long fingers reveal an artistic, aesthetic and intellectual nature, while shorter fingers foretell a practical and physically active child. The palm of the hand relates to your baby's physical constitution. If the palm is longer than the fingers, the baby will have a strong, persevering nature. A thick palm shows that the baby will generally have a healthy and adventurous life. A wide palm indicates that the baby is strong and full of vitality.

The shape of your baby's head when he is first delivered may be slightly unbalanced; the birthing process exerts huge pressures on your baby's skull and these bones are not yet fixed in place. The head will return to its natural shape within a few days and will be more fixed after about one month. All babies have soft spots – fontanelles – on the top of their heads. The normal time period for the bones of the skull to fuse and for the fontanelles to close is 6–18 months. If you look more closely at his head, you may notice that one side is slightly larger. If the left side is more developed, your baby has the potential to have an intellectual and idealistic nature. On the other hand, a more pronounced right side indicates a practical and down-to-earth character.

Patterns of hair vary from baby to baby. Usually, at the top of a baby's head is a spiral. If this spiral is fairly central, he will have a balanced, well-rounded nature. If it is on the right side, he will tend to have a socially and physically active nature, whereas if the spiral sits on the left then he'll be more intellectual. Sometimes, a baby has a double spiral. In this case he will develop a unique character but care must be taken that he isn't attracted to extremes, be they food or lifestyle. If the back of your baby's head is prominent, he has a well-developed cerebellum, often called the 'small brain'. He may develop the tendency to be more active, determined and sometimes quite outspoken.

The eyes represent the entire mental, physical and spiritual condition of your baby – like windows to the world – and reflect his inner nature. If he has close-set eyes, he may have an emotionally and intellectually sharp nature but can be stubborn. If the eyes are widely spaced, he will have a more gentle character but may have trouble making decisions.

The eyebrows reflect the history of a baby's time in the womb. The course of life mirrors development during pregnancy, and so eyebrows indicate your baby's destiny. Downward-slanting eyebrows indicate a gentle, understanding nature. If the eyebrows slant upwards, he will tend towards a strong, somewhat aggressive character. Smooth arched eyebrows indicate that he will be well balanced and adaptable.

The nose reflects your baby's nervous and circulatory system. The shape of the nose corresponds to the size, quality and condition of his brain. Large nostrils are considered more masculine and show a strong, vital and active personality. Small feminine nostrils are artistic and

There was a little girl,
and she had a little curl
right in the middle of her forehead;
When she was good,
she was very very good
but when she was bad, she was horrid.

gentle. An upwards-pointing nose indicates sharp thinking but can also reflect narrow-mindedness. A nose that droops downwards indicates a gentle character. A slightly large nose is associated with an open mind.

The ears represent the entire physical and mental constitution of your baby. Ears that are flat against the head indicate an ability to understand many points of view and the potential for good social skills. If the outer rim of the ear is thick, it shows that your baby has a caring, compassionate nature. A well-developed flap of cartilage at the front of the ear indicates strength, perseverance and tolerance.

The mouth shows the general quality of the digestive system. It should be pinkish-red in colour, indicating high blood quality and good circulation. If the central part of the lips is clearly shaped, your baby will have vitality and perseverance. If he has a full mouth he will often be outwardly expressive. Thin lips show that when he can talk your child may have difficulty expressing deep feelings.

The Tooth Fairy

The myths and legends that surround fairies are extremely varied but it is generally viewed that their world is full of magical power and enchantment. Everything is possible in the land of the fairies, and the creative force that we feel is the very one that makes up their world. Theirs is a secret world of joy, love, the invisible, humour, mischief, tragedy and mystical enchantments.

Fairies have the ability to transform themselves and are difficult to meet because they resent the clumsy intrusions of humans. The lighter spirit and natural innocence of children makes it easier for them to align with the fairy world. The tooth fairy is a distant cousin of those spirits that belong to the woods, meadows and the sea. She is known throughout the world and belongs to no specific religion. Each and every child on earth can be visited by the mysteriously nocturnal tooth fairy.

The loss of baby teeth marks a big step in your child's life and represents the beginning of independence. Children love to mark this event by placing their teeth under their pillows for the tooth fairy to take away. She leaves a gift in its place. Most tooth fairies leave a small monetary surprise but it is also possible for her to leave a small stone, crystal or even a little charm to mark the occasion.

Choose or make a holder for your infant's tooth to be held safely in, under the pillow, ready and waiting for the tooth fairy to arrive. These include tiny and sometimes very ornate boxes, small dolls with tooth pockets, silk pouches and hand-painted envelopes.

Children are thrilled by the world of imagination. They love to listen to stories of things that cannot be seen or explained in real terms. The tooth fairy is one of those special characters that gives childhood a sense of wonder and delight. For a child, waking up the next morning is incredibly exciting and to find that the tooth fairy has left a gift of some kind reinforces the magic and mystery of this very special visitor.

When the first baby laughed for the first time,
the laugh broke into a thousand pieces
and they all went skipping about,
and that was the beginning of fairies.

Your Baby's Birth Record

provides a special place to mark your baby's arrival into the world. Although you're unlikely to forget such a momentous day, keeping a record of all his details, along with any poems or blessings you want to give him, is a wondrous keepsake that you can refer to in years to come.

Birthday Details

TIME
....

DAY
....

MONTH
....

YEAR
....

DOCTOR
....

ALSO PRESENT AT THE BIRTH
....

....

Vital Statistics

BABY'S FULL NAME
....

....

WEIGHT
....

LENGTH
....

HEAD CIRCUMFERENCE
....

DISTINGUISHING MARKS
....

EYE COLOUR
....

HAIR COLOUR
....

Record your feelings about your baby's birth …

Your Baby's...

...footprints

...handprints

...lock of hair

Write a poem/blessing here to welcome your baby into the world ...

I would like to thank my children who have taught me the most in my life: Alisa, Madeline, Amy, Zoe, Andrew, Natasha, Sam and my step-children Nathan, Joseph and Naomi. A big thanks to my teachers and colleagues who opened my eyes to a beautiful way of living: Michio and Aveline Kushi, Shizuko Yamamoto, Denny Waxman, Judith Flohr, Saul Goodman, Michelle Nemer, Susan Goodwin, Diane Avoli, Chico and Eugenia Varatojo.

A special thank you to my family who have always been there for me: Simon and Dragana Brown and their children, Adam and Angela Brown and the girls, and Marilyn, Joshua, Erin, Alaina, Jenny, Mathew and Howard Waxman. Thanks to my friends who have given me so much love and encouragement: Helen Stevenson, Deborah Albaneze, Susan Reid, Jean and Amanda Schearer, Michael Kabbeko, Joe Magnotta, Michael Maloney, Natasha Novoselova, Boy George, John and Maria Brosnan and my friends at the Avante salon and spa.

I would also like to thank all the mothers and babies who have shown me the wonder of new life and to everyone at Carroll & Brown, especially Amy Carroll and Nikki Sims.

Melanie Waxman

Carroll and Brown would like to thank the following for providing images:

Prêt A Vivre	www.pretavivre.com (telephone 020 8960 6111)
	email: sales@pretavivre.com
The White Company	www.thewhiteco.com (customer services 0870 160 1610)

pages 42 (top), *69, 87, 95, 103, 105* The White Company
page 30 Telegraph Colour Library
page 37 John Wilkes/Photonica
page 67 Getty Images Stone
page 81 David Murray
page 90 The Stock Market
Front jacket Getty Images Stone